DATE DUE	

Other titles in the Briefcase Books series include:

Customer Relationship Management
by Kristin Anderson and Carol Kerr

Communicating Effectively by Lani Arredondo

Performance Management by Robert Bacal

Recognizing and Rewarding Employees by R. Brayton Bowen

Six Sigma for Managers by Greg Brue

Motivating Employees by Anne Bruce and James S. Pepitone

Leadership Skills for Managers by Marlene Caroselli

Negotiating Skills for Managers by Steven Cohen

Effective Coaching by Marshall J. Cook

Conflict Resolution by Daniel Dana

Project Management by Gary R. Heerkens

Managing Teams by Lawrence Holpp

Hiring Great People by Kevin C. Klinvex,
Matthew S. O'Connell, and Christopher P. Klinvex

Retaining Top Employees by J. Leslie McKeown

Empowering Employees by Kenneth L. Murrell and Mimi
Meredith

Presentation Skills for Managers, by Jennifer Rotondo
and Mike Rotondo

The Manager's Guide to Business Writing
by Suzanne D. Sparks

Skills for New Managers by Morey Stettner

Manager's Survival Guide by Morey Stettner

Managing Multiple Projects by Michael Tobis and Irene P. Tobis

To learn more about titles in the Briefcase Books series go to
www.briefcasebooks.com
You'll find the tables of contents, downloadable sample chapters, information on the authors, discussion guides for using these books in training programs, and more.

A
Briefcase
Book

Interviewing Techniques for Managers

Carolyn B. Thompson

McGraw-Hill

New York Chicago San Francisco Lisbon London
Madrid Mexico City Milan New Delhi San Juan
Seoul Singapore Sydney Toronto

Copyright © 2002 by The McGraw-Hill Companies, Inc. All rights reserved.
Printed in the United States of America. Except as permitted under the
United States Copyright Act of 1976, no part of this publication may be
reproduced or distributed in any form or by any means, or stored in a data-
base or retrieval system, without the prior written permission of the publisher.

1 2 3 4 5 6 7 8 9 0 AGM/AGM 0 9 8 7 6 5 4 3 2

ISBN 0-07-139131-2

Library of Congress Cataloging-in-Publication Data applied for.

This is a CWL Publishing Enterprises Book, *developed and produced for
McGraw-Hill by* CWL Publishing Enterprises, Madison, WI, *www.cwlpub.com.*

This publication is designed to provide accurate and authoritative information in regard to the subject matter covered. It is sold with the understanding
that neither the author nor the publisher is engaged in rendering legal,
accounting, or other professional service. If legal advice or other expert
assistance is required, the services of a competent professional person
should be sought.
        *—From a Declaration of Principles jointly adopted by a Committee
        of the American Bar Association and a Committee of Publishers*

McGraw-Hill books are available at special quantity discounts to use as pre-
miums and sales promotions, or for use in corporate training programs. For
more information, please write to the Director of Special Sales, McGraw-Hill,
2 Penn Plaza, New York, NY 10128. Or contact your local bookstore.

 This book is printed on recycled, acid-free paper containing a minimum of 50% recycled de-inked fiber.

Contents

Preface   ix

1. **Why Am I Interviewing?**   **1**
   Behavioral Interviewing   1
   Interviewing: It's Not Just Asking Questions   9
   Skills for Successful Interviews   11
   Steps in Any Interview   12
   Manager's Checklist for Chapter 1   16

2. **How Can I Connect with the Person I'm Interviewing?**   **17**
   How to Use the Platinum Rule   19
   Discover Your Communication Style   20
   Recognizing Communication Styles and
      Modifying to Adapt   25
   Caution: Contents Under Pressure!   35
   Planning to Modify Your Way of Communicating   38
   Planning to Gain Information from People
      Who Are Different from You   39
   Manager's Checklist for Chapter 2   43

3. **What Questions Should I Ask—and How?**   **45**
   What Types of Questions Should You Ask?   45
   How to Decide What Questions You'll Ask   57
   How Should You Ask the Questions?   60
   Manager's Checklist for Chapter 3   66

4. **How Should I Plan for the Interview?**   **68**
   Setting Objectives   70
   Determining and Setting the Environment   78

Determining and Setting the Plan: Agenda and Methods   86
Manager's Checklist for Chapter 4   90

5. **How Should I Prepare for the Interview?**   **91**
Gathering Information Before the Interview   91
What to Communicate in Advance to Prepare the Person   93
Creating and Using the Interview Tools   96
Legal Issues   101
Putting It All Together   108
Manager's Checklist for Chapter 5   108

6. **How Should I Begin and End the Interview?**   **109**
The Beginning: Gaining Attention and Creating Comfort   112
The Ending: Gaining Commitment   127
Manager's Checklist for Chapter 6   130

7. **What Are They Saying ... and Conveying?**   **131**
Active Listening   132
What Are You Listening For?   134
Active Listening Behaviors   139
Getting Rid of Barriers to Listening   148
Manager's Checklist for Chapter 7   151

8. **What if They Don't Act Like I Expect?**   **153**
Six Difficult Behaviors   155
Behaviors, Possible Causes, and Your Response   157
Figuring Out the Causes   162
Avoiding Negative Emotions   171
Manager's Checklist for Chapter 8   174

9. **How Do I Use Technology Successfully?**   **175**
What's Different When Conducting Interviews
    Using Technology?   176
Telephone, Conference Calls, and Videoconferencing   179
Web   184
E-mail and Instant Messaging   187
Audio- and Videotaping   191
Manager's Checklist for Chapter 9   192

10. **How Do I Use the Information I've Gathered?**   **194**
Methods for Clarifying When You Need Additional
    Information After the Interview   196
Making Decisions with the Information   200

Communicating the Decision and Creating a
    Positive Feeling About Your Organization   201
Continuously Improving Your Interviewing Skills   207
Manager's Checklist for Chapter 10   210

Index   **211**

Preface

Be honest: the first reaction to the word "interviewing" is what? Employee hiring. Yes, like the almost everybody in the world, we hear or read the word "interviewing" and we think "employment."

Interviewing is simply getting information from another person. We all use this skill every day. In fact, most days you'll be involved in at least 10 interviews a day—ones you initiate and ones initiated by others. Every time you work at getting information from customers about the problem they're having, you're interviewing. Every time you talk with a potential customer to learn his or her needs, you're interviewing. In every performance appraisal conversation that includes gaining information from your employee, you're interviewing. Every time you talk with your colleagues in other companies to learn how they do things, you're interviewing. Every time you discuss with your coworkers while planning a project or determining the strategic plan for the company, you're interviewing. And, of course, every time you gain information from potential employees and volunteers, you're interviewing.

It's a bit of a twist. This book focuses on interviewing skills—information-gaining skills—in every situation. If you're in Customer Service, the steps and skills you'll learn will help you gain information from customers. If you're in Human Resources, Marketing, Sales, Volunteer Management, Operations, Finance, or IS, this book will help you make it easy and enjoyable for your direct employees, coworkers, customers, and colleagues to give you the information you need.

As I wrote, I struggled (no pity, please—it was great fun!) to balance the "just the facts" style of Briefcase Books with the need to give you examples for all types of gaining information from others. No matter what managerial responsibilities you hold, I wanted you to see yourself and the type of information gaining you do as you read each step and worked on each skill. To do this, as you'll see, I wrote examples for each person and situation in which you'd interview and/or I made the description of each step in the interviewing process so generic that you'd feel like this applied to you and the people you interview.

You'll also notice that I know something about each of you—you're incredibly busy and you'll read just the chapters you feel you needed. Look at the table of contents. The chapters are the steps to successful interviewing, in order. Reading chapters here and there as you need them quite obviously will cause you to miss some of the steps you need to take to gain the information you need. So, each chapter is full of references to pages in the book where you'll find those steps.

Every interviewing step and every example uses behavioral interviewing techniques, rather than interviewing with hypothetical questions. Why? Because you'll get the information you need faster and it'll be more accurate and more detailed. Why? Because behavioral interviewing leads you to talk with people about themselves! You'll be talking with them about things that happened to them, things they've done and how they've done them.

Interviewing Techniques for Managers will help you plan and prepare for any interview, conduct the all-important opening and closing of any information-gaining session, and use the information you gain to make decisions. You'll get methods for communicating with different people in a way that makes it easy for them to understand, creating questions, listening, taking notes, and dealing with people who seem bent on making it difficult to get the information from them. The book is full of ready-to-use forms, tools, and checklists to make it easy for you to gain information from anyone quickly, accurately, and in a way that makes them feel great about you and your organization.

Special Features

The idea behind the books in the Briefcase Series is to give you practical information written in a friendly person-to-person style. The chapters are short, deal with tactical issues, and include lots of examples. They also feature numerous sidebars designed to give you different types of specific information. Here's a description of these sidebars and how they're used in this book.

Boxes with this icon are designed to give you tips and tactics that will help you more effectively implement the methods described in this book.

These boxes provide warnings for where things could go wrong in planning and carrying out your interviews.

These boxes highlight insider tips for taking advantage of the techniques described in this book.

Every subject has some special jargon and terms. These boxes provide definitions of these concepts.

It's always important to have examples of what others have done, either well or not so well. Find these stories in these boxes.

This identifies boxes where you'll find specific procedures you can follow to take advantage of the book's advice.

How can you make sure you won't make a mistake when managing? You can't, but these boxes will give you practical advice on how to minimize the possibility.

Acknowledgments

Incredible thanks to John Woods and Robert Magnan of CWL Publishing. Bob's editing really helped to create a great balance between examples you'd need in order to understand what to do and examples that just took up space (the ultimate storyteller, I couldn't help myself). You can actually find what you need in this book and read it because of John's terrific formatting and layout. Left to my own devices, I'd have everything you needed to know on one piece of paper: it would be huge and not very practical—but I hate turning pages.

Interviewing Techniques for Managers

Why Am I Interviewing?

I think it is important to learn as much as you can about everything around you. I truly believe that knowledge is the key to being successful in life.
　　　　　　　—Connie Chung

The first step in interviewing is to ask yourself the question that serves as title of this chapter—Why am I interviewing?

We interview to learn, to gain knowledge. We need to get information from another person. It's an interactive process that takes a certain skill. That's the purpose of this book, to help you develop that skill.

Behavioral Interviewing

The fastest, most accurate method to gain knowledge from another person and, incidentally, the easiest way for the other person to give it is a process called *behavioral interviewing.* All of the techniques we present in this book will use this process. (We argued over whether you'd want to learn slower,

Interview A meeting at which one person obtains information from another. A manager may need to interview candidates for employment or volunteer work, his or her direct employees, peers, current and potential customers, vendors, and managers in other organizations.

less accurate ways of interviewing and figured we'd skip those!)

In behavioral interviewing, we always ask questions relating to something the person has done or something that happened to him or her, as opposed to hypothetical examples.

So, for example, we'd ask, "Tell me what you did when you had a coworker who didn't get their part of the project done," as opposed to "If a coworker doesn't get their part of a project done, what will you do?"

Behavioral interviewing A process that is based on the premise that the most accurate predictor of future performance is past performance in a similar situation. Behavioral interviewing focuses on examples of past behavior that can be used to predict future actions, attitudes, and/or needs. It is a systematic process that is structured and goal-oriented. Behavioral interviewing was born in the employment interview arena. It was originally developed in the 1970s by Development Dimensions International, Inc. (DDI) and called Targeted Selection.

Read the first of the two questions again: "Tell me what you did when you had a coworker who didn't get their part of the project done." As you're reading the question, you're thinking about a coworker who didn't get a project done. It's immediate. It's automatic. Our brain thinks in pictures and as the interviewer is saying the sentence your brain is painting the picture.

Now read the second of the two questions again: "If a coworker doesn't get their part of a project done, what will you do?" Nothing. No pictures. While the interviewer is saying the sentence, your mind is blank. After the interviewer finishes, you review the question in your mind. Then you think, "Hmmm, when has something like that happened?" Then you review what happened. Then you start talking. By this time the interviewer is writing notes like "slow thinker."

Or, after reviewing the question in your mind, you think, "Hmmm, I wonder what they mean. I wonder what they're looking for. I wonder how I should answer this?" Then, assuming you're cool in test situations, you think about what you're going to say. Then you start saying what you think they want to hear.

If you're not good in test situations, you'll do one of two things: you'll start talking without thinking and do a lot of ummming and hmmmming and pausing because you're thinking and talking at the same time or you'll get so flustered you can't answer—and then even more flustered because you can't answer.

Does either of the responses to the second question suggest that the interview will go well and you'll get the information you want? Not really!

The first question, in contrast, makes the other person feel comfortable. He or she is giving me details, providing the information I need fast—at least faster than the person who was asked the second question and who's still thinking, fumbling, and rambling.

You can get the information faster and it'll be more accurate, more detailed, and come from someone who's feeling confident because you asked a question he or she can answer. It's about the person. It's about something that happened to the person. It's not about something hypothetical, something that he or she

---

Avoid the "I Word"

CAUTION!

The word "interview" may provoke a negative gut reaction. We usually think of our experiences trying to get jobs or of media folks such as Barbara Walters, Diane Sawyer, Connie Chung, or Sam Donaldson. Does the word "interview" make us feel comfortable? Probably not. So it's generally best to avoid using the "I word" with people. Call it a "talk" or a "conversation" or even a "discussion." As much as we may want to believe what Juliet told Romeo, "That which we call a rose by any other name would smell as sweet," when you use the "I word" you're working against years of associations that may not all be pleasant.

might do or that may happen to him or her.

Make the interview easy and enjoyable and it'll be easy for the person you're interviewing to give you the information you need. You'll save time and get more accurate information—and both of you will feel better about the experience.

You're sold. Behavioral interviewing—getting people to give you information about things they've done or that have happened to them—is the way to go. Now, let's look at the people with whom you would use behavioral interviewing, some typical situations, and examples that show how it works.

This will be just a brief introduction to behavioral interviewing, to show how you can use it to get information from people for various purposes, in various situations. In the chapters to follow, we'll get to all the steps of planning and preparing, conducting, and documenting interviews and then using the results.

Candidates for Employment or Volunteer Work

Situation: When you're assessing a person for the right fit with your organization, the tasks, and the method by which the tasks need to done.

How It Works. You've just listened to a voice mail from a candidate for the telephone sales position. The process you planned for finding the right employee starts with candidates telling you in voice mail why their skills would meet your needs (which they read on your Web site). This person said all the things you were looking for, but he paused many times and the quality of his voice was high-pitched. Was the person nervous because it's part of his job interview or is that his normal pace and pitch? Pauses and a high pitch quality will make prospects for your company's services feel less than confident about the salesperson, a feeling that translates to the company and your services. You'll need to find out whether he can speak without so many pauses and in a lower-pitched voice. So, when you call, you'll be attentive to his pace and pitch.

Here's what you say:

Describe a time when you felt nervous during a phone call with a prospective customer—and tell me the ways you think you exhibited the nervousness.

(*He gives an example.*)

I notice you pause frequently within and between sentences. Are you pausing for emphasis, to prepare your next thought so it'll come out like you meant it, or for another reason?

Your Direct Employees

Situation: When you're conducting the annual performance appraisal, in day-to-day coaching, and in career development and planning.

You need to gain information from your employee in order to know about his or her goals, plans, and needs. In these situations, you'll look at examples of past behavior and use them to predict and plan the future actions, attitudes, and needs that will allow them to succeed.

How It Works. One of your employees has asked you about her potential for a promotion in the company. She's been with you for a year and a half and from day one she's clearly communicated her expectation of moving up to manage projects or people. Though her next performance appraisal isn't due for a few months, you agree to meet with her and discuss her situation. She is really capable in her current job, when she focuses her attention, and you feel she has the ambition to succeed as a manager. The thing that's holding you back from recommending her for promotion is that she hurries through most tasks. Maybe she feels some of the tasks aren't challenging enough, so she hurries through them to get to others. Whatever the reason, she makes more mistakes when she's hurrying than others in the department who aren't as capable. You'll need to find out why she hurries and what's causing her to make mistakes on certain types of work, so you can help her figure out what to do to be promotable.

Here's what you say:

Name all your favorite tasks.

(After she does, if she names any tasks in which she's made mistakes, do the following for each one.)

You like ... and last week you *(describe the specific mistake)*. What was happening that day when you were working on ....?

Peers

Situation: When you're involved in annual strategic planning for the organization or department, planning a project, or ongoing problem solving.

By using a systematic process that is structured and goal-oriented, you get information faster and you make it easier to set the plans together and discover problems and then take action on those problems.

How It Works. You and two members of your work group are meeting to develop the rationale part of a plan for purchasing a new piece of equipment. You start by stating the objective for the meeting—to determine and write the rationale for purchasing the equipment so it can be presented to management. You have only 10 minutes, so you need to be succinct but cover all the bases. Your job is to get as much information from the work group members as possible so you can produce the most compelling rationale. To start, you'll need to know how the equipment will be used, how much it'll be used, and how long it will be usable.

Here's what you say:

List every use of this piece of equipment you've read about, discussed with the manufacturer, or planned yourself.

What did the manufacturer tell us that other companies using the equipment in the ways we've just listed have found to be their maximum and minimum number of hours of use each day?

Name the areas we have to take into account to determine length of usability. What did the manufacturer say that other companies had experienced in each of these areas?

Current and Potential Customers

Situation: When you're working with a potential customer in the one-on-one sales process or structured focus groups to discover their needs or with current customers to discover needs and solve problems.

You'll benefit here from the steps of the behavioral interviewing process:

- planning and preparing
- beginning the interview (conversation)
- asking and answering questions
- listening
- documenting
- ending to gain commitment
- analysis of their information in order to make the sale or take care of a problem to the satisfaction of your customer

How It Works. A new customer has placed his first order. You were eager to get his business, so you OK'd a shorter deadline than usual for the order. The customer had to have it by Friday. Now it's Friday and the customer calls and asks for you. He tells you that he received only part of the order. He explains that he told the person who took his order that he had to have it by Friday and the person assured him that, even though it was short notice, he would receive it on time. He's angry.

When you receive the call, you aren't aware of any delay or back orders. You'll have to find out how this problem happened and see what can be done to get the customer his order and save the new account. But first you need some information from the customer.

Here's what you say:

I'm really sorry that we were unable to get your entire order to you as we'd promised. Now, I'll be able to help you do what you need to get done if I know what day, what time, and where you'll need to be using the ....

(*If you can't get him something that will work for him, based on your new knowledge, and you want offer him an incentive to try you again, say the following.*)

I'm very sorry. We really want to prove to you that we can meet your needs the next time. Please tell me what other companies have done in this situation that caused you to try them the next time.

Vendors and Managers in Other Organizations

Situation: When you're assessing vendors' products and services or benchmarking the practices of your colleagues' organizations.

Use behavioral interviewing to make it easy for them to give you the information you need to decide whose products to buy, whose services to use, or what changes to make to your organization's practices.

How It Works. You need to hire a training company to help your staff learn the new software that they're scheduled to start using in a month. The original plan was to learn from the manuals, but during beta testing it was obvious that your staff needed an expert. You call a few colleagues and one recommends a company that she brought in to help her staff. She was very pleased with the company's ability to put together and facilitate training that created an easy and relatively unobtrusive way for her employees to learn their new software.

You just can't imagine how the trainers could learn your massive software package fast enough to make this happen. Obviously you'll need to find out, among other things, how they'll be able to help your people learn the software within the month, what method of training will be the best for your situation, and how much it'll cost.

Here's what you say:

My colleague tells me you helped her in the middle of an implementation. What steps did you follow to learn her software so you could help her staff learn it?

Tell me what you need to know from us so you can create the best method of learning for our situation.

What did you charge my colleague and in what ways is our situation similar to hers?

Interviewing: It's Not Just Asking Questions

Most of us are used to gaining information from others by using questions. However, few interview objectives will be met solely by questions, since some of the things you need to know are more accurately learned through other methods, for any of several reasons:

- The people you'll be interviewing may not want to give you accurate information and they're good at answering questions in ways that will put the best spin on their information.
- The people you'll be interviewing are poor communicators.
- The information you need can only be seen (their writing style, their speed on a particular task, a product that's broken, how they use the product, how something works for other organizations).

You want to make it easy for the person to give you the information you need. Here are some methods that allow you to gain more accurate information and get it faster in various situations:

1. You send the person questions in writing in advance of the interview and ask him or her to read them and maybe also write answers to the questions. In that case, the person then brings the answers to the interview and the two of you discuss them. This method is incredibly helpful for people who need to think ahead to feel sure about what they're telling you. Have someone read your written questions first, to make sure the person will understand them.
2. You bring to the interview some document (e.g., a direct employee's Friday report, a candidate's file on a diskette,

a vendor's schematic of an installation) and the two of you discuss it. If you're sharing a single document (no copies), there's more interaction.

3. Ask the person to read information about the organization, job, service, or product and/or to watch a video, visit a Web site, use a CD, or listen to audio. Then, during the interview, ask for any questions, impressions, or ideas. This method works great for situations like problem solving, where people feel more comfortable having time to think before meeting to discuss. Never use this approach solely as a way to provide information; you'd be missing the opportunity to gain information from the reactions of the person to that information.

4. Have the person experience something—perform a task or use a product/service in front of you, watch others do it in person, watch a video of it being done, participate in a role-play or simulation, read or listen to a case study about it being done, and so forth. Then discuss what the person learned, what ideas he or she now has, or what he or she needs to change. The more real the experience, the more accurate the information you'll get, so use actual tasks, products, or services when possible. (Before you use this method, read the "Legal Issues" section of Chapter 5.)

5. Have the person take paper or computer tests of aptitude, interests, and/or needs. Use commercial, normed tests for the greatest validity and least expense. Creating your own that will be valid is much more expensive; creating your own that aren't validated will not only give you less accurate information but also possibly expose you to claims of discrimination. (Read Chapter 5, "Legal Issues.")

6. Take the person on a tour of a location or to meet other employees or customers to experience specific things and then discuss reactions and any ideas or questions. Prepare staff for this, either in general—"This could happen at any time in your employment with us and this is why we include this type of thing in interviews here"—or specific to this interview. When it's specific, tell them when, who, and why

you're interviewing, what their role is, and what you'll want to know from them later.

Skills for Successful Interviews

Listed in the box starting on the next page are the skills needed to be successful with the behavioral interviewing process. You may already excel in some areas; in that case, you can use the ideas in this book so you can really excel. In other areas, you'll need to build up your skills. Always work on both excelling and improving—many times excellence in one skill can compensate for deficiencies in another.

Use this checklist now to plan how you'll use this book to excel in gaining information from others and creating a positive feeling about the experience.

I excel	I could improve	
❑	❑	Using active listening skills *(Chapter 7)*
❑	❑	Thinking on your feet *(Chapters 2, 6, 8)*
❑	❑	Flexibility *(Chapters 2, 3, 6, 7, 8, 9, 10)*
❑	❑	Ability to plan for the interview quickly and thoroughly *(Chapters 4, 5)*
❑	❑	Ability to organize, compare, and analyze information *(Chapters 2, 4, 5, 7, 10)*
❑	❑	Knowledge of your organization, service, or product *(Chapter 6)*
❑	❑	Belief in your organization, service, or product *(Chapters 6, 10)*
❑	❑	Ability to provide a win-win outcome *(Chapters 8, 10)*
❑	❑	Scheduling and doing follow-up carefully and accurately *(Chapter 10)*
❑	❑	Love of interacting with people *(Chapters 2, 8)*
❑	❑	Persistence *(Chapters 3, 7, 8, 9)*
❑	❑	Thorough documentation *(Chapters 4, 5, 7)*
❑	❑	Ability to create a good impression for yourself and your organization *(Chapter 6)*
❑	❑	Ability to help the person you're interviewing understand the benefits for him or her *(Chapter 6)*

I excel	I could improve	
❑	❑	Ability to help the person you're interviewing understand what you need from him or her *(Chapter 6)*
❑	❑	Ability to research quickly and thoroughly *(Chapters 4, 5)*
❑	❑	Being able to feel positive very quickly after rejection or an error *(Chapter 8)*
❑	❑	Using a voice that the person you're interviewing interprets as enthusiastic *(Chapters 2, 3, 6, 7, 8, 9)*
❑	❑	Knowing the way the person you're interviewing likes to be communicated with *(Chapter 2)*
❑	❑	Understanding the time limits of the person you're interviewing *(Chapters 2, 4, 5, 6)*
❑	❑	Ability to speak and write effectively *(Chapters 3, 6, 7, 8, 10)*

Steps in Any Interview

There are five steps common to any behavioral interview you undertake. They are

- Plan and prepare for the interview
- Begin the interview with objectives
- Gather information and document it (talking, listening, writing)
- End the interview in a way that gains commitment
- Use the information gained to make decisions/take action

An interview will be most successful if you follow all the

So, What's the Point?

Set your objective(s) for the interview. Be specific and focus on the action you want to be able to take as a result of the interview. Your objective is to get the information you need to do something specific. When you can specify how you want to use the information, you make it easier to get the information you need. Or, as baseball great Yogi Berra put it, "You've got to be very careful if you don't know where you're going, because you might not get there."

steps. If, however, you
miss a part of the interview
process, you can still gain
information by compensat-

Objective A specific end
toward which we direct
some specific effort.

ing for the part missing, but it takes lots of hard work and practice. It just makes more sense, then, to execute all of the steps
of the interview process, so that everything goes as efficiently
and effectively as possible.

Without planning and preparing, for example, it's difficult to
begin the interview with objectives, to gather information, or
end in a way that gains commitment, because we don't have an
objective clear enough to state, we don't have the questions
determined in advance, we don't have a way to record the information (no form), and we don't have an ending planned. We
compensate for the lack of planning by spending more time in
the interview, figuring out what we're doing as we go. After a
while, we develop an ability to "think on our feet" so that we
may not seem to be unprepared and we may muddle through
better, but it still takes longer and therefore we won't receive
some of the benefits of planning.

The same is true for the other steps. If we don't start by stating the objectives, we lose time because the interview is less
focused. If we don't use our interview information-gathering tool
to record information, we'll have a hard time making a decision
and/or using the information later. If we don't end the interview
in a way that gains commitment, we don't achieve the maximum results for our efforts. Finally, if we don't use the information we've gained to make decisions and/or take action, then
why did we even do the interview?

All the parts of the behavioral interviewing process are important. They work together to help you achieve your objectives.

Plan and Prepare for the Interview

Abraham Lincoln said, "If I had eight hours to chop down a tree,
I'd spend six sharpening my ax." "Plan" is a four-letter word for
most of us. But planning for an interview can often save time

and it almost always results in a better interview.

We'll need to plan our objectives for the interview and how we'll prepare the environment to minimize distractions and make the other person feel comfortable. We'll need to choose the steps for deciding who we'll interview, how we'll notify them, and how much time we'll need for the interview. We'll also need to gather as much information as possible in advance, so we're aware of what we don't know and can prepare our questions. Planning is never complete until you know what you'll do with the information—how you'll assess it to make decisions and/or take action to meet your objectives. We'll get into planning and preparing in Chapter 4 and, to some extent, in Chapters 2 and 3.

Begin the Interview with Objectives

This part of the interview is relatively easy—and we can really undermine our efforts if we neglect it.

We always have two kinds of objectives for any interview: to get information and to leave the other person feeling a certain way after the interview. (When we discuss planning, we'll get more specific about both objectives.)

It's crucial to state the *information* objective in every interview. It focuses all the participants on a similar picture of the outcome/end of the interview: a meeting is just a gathering of bodies if there's no meeting of the minds. We'll discuss this part of the interview in Chapter 6.

The *feeling* objective, on the other hand, is usually not stated. But it's important to monitor it throughout the interview and make adjustments as necessary.

> **TRICKS OF THE TRADE**
>
> ### Read the Reaction
> Begin working toward your *feeling* objective from the first moments of the interview. When you state your *information* objective, pay close attention to the reaction of the other person. That reaction (verbal and/or nonverbal) will reveal how well or poorly his or her objective aligns with yours—and suggest ways to bring the person to feeling a certain way by the end of the interview.

Gather Information and Document It

This is the heart of the interview. This is where you benefit from planning and preparing and from establishing the objectives. But there's a lot going on and the interaction takes many skills, as we'll outline and explain in Chapter 7. If you've planned and prepared properly, you can make almost any interview seem as comfortable as a casual conversation.

End the Interview in a Way That Gains Commitment

Once you've achieved the objectives, it's time to end the interview. It's not just a matter of picking up your things and walking away from the table. You use the ending that you planned in Chapter 4 for the most effective conclusion, a conclusion that achieves your unstated objective, to leave the other person feeling a certain way after the interview and gain some commitment from the person.

Commitment is essential: without it, you're left unsure about using the information you gained—what decisions do you need to make and what actions do you need to take if the other person isn't committed? We'll discuss ending the interview in Chapter 6.

Use the Information Gained to Make Decisions and/or Take Action

Finally, we make decisions and/or take action based on the information we documented with the interview information-gathering tool. We have our objectives, we have information, and we can now weigh all the information against the objectives and prioritize possible decisions and/or actions.

The follow-up after the interview is where all our efforts pay off: we offer the

> **Succeed Through Skills and Structure** *Smart Managing*
>
> There are two fundamentals for interviewing effectively and efficiently:
> * Assess your interviewing skill areas and work to excel or improve in all areas.
> * Know and use all the parts of the behavioral interviewing process.

position, we fix the problem, we get the service or product, we achieve the plan, the employee improves, and so forth. In the process we may need to answer a few more clarifying questions or to restate what we agreed on in order to finalize the commitment. We will keep the positive feeling going if we've been meeting that objective all along—or we will kill it if we don't follow up. These final matters are the focus of Chapter 10.

Manager's Checklist for Chapter 1

❏ The fastest, most accurate method to gain knowledge from another person and, incidentally, the easiest way for the other person to give it is a process called *behavioral interviewing*.

❏ Use the behavioral interviewing process for candidates for employment or volunteer work, your direct employees, your peers, current and potential customers, vendors, and managers in other organizations.

❏ Consider methods other than asking questions in situations where alternative approaches would allow you to get more accurate information more efficiently.

❏ Always work on the skills you're great at so you can excel while building up the skills you're not quite great at. Many times excellence in one area compensates for deficiencies in another area.

How Can I Connect with the Person I'm Interviewing?

The Platinum Rule: "Do unto others as they would have you do unto them."

Have you found yourself in verbal struggles with someone you're interviewing as you try to drag the information from him or her? Does it take several attempts with a certain customer to convince that person of the merits of your idea? Can you think of a time when the person said one thing to you and later did something very different?

We walk away from these interactions thinking, "This person doesn't want to give me the information" or "This person doesn't want to buy my product" or "This person changed what they led me to believe." Though there are certainly people you'll interview who do want to withhold information, don't want to buy, or do tell untruths, effective communication will often take care of such situations.

Whose job is it to communicate effectively with the person you're interviewing? Yours! So, how do you do that? Recognize how the other person likes to communicate and then modify your way of talking with them to fit his or hers.

You'll get the information you need from people easily because they'll understand what you're asking them and feel so comfortable they'll want to give it to you. If you use the Platinum Rule as part of the method by which you communicate in behavioral interviewing, it will help you hire the best person for the job, discover the real problem quickly, learn more from people, and discover needs you can meet by "knowing" the person you're interviewing even if you've never met!

You remember the Golden Rule—"Do unto others as you would have them do unto you"? Many of us, as children, learned this model for good behavior and we apply it to our communication. That's great for behavior, but the Platinum Rule is infinitely more effective for communication: "Do unto others as *they* would have you do unto them." This simple principle revolutionized my ability to understand what people really were telling me and get them to easily give me the information I needed.

Any time you interview someone, there are at least two parties, the sender and the receiver. It is always, always, always the sender's responsibility to make sure the receiver gets the information the way he or she needs it in order to take it in easily and understand.

Do you know someone you love to talk with because it's easy to understand what that person means—no hidden meanings, no asking a bunch of questions to get him or her to be more specific, no long boring descriptions you don't need? You can be like that for people you interview—and you can save time and avoid frustration because you make it easy for them to give you the information you need.

Figure 2-1 lists what successful interviewers do—most, if not all, through communication. When you "know" the person you're interviewing, you can communicate the way he or she is most comfortable.

- Using active listening skills
- Thinking on your feet
- Flexibility
- Ability to plan for the interview quickly and thoroughly
- Ability to organize, compare, and analyze information
- Knowledge of your organization, service, or product
- Belief in your organization, service, or product
- Ability to provide a win-win outcome
- Scheduling and doing follow-up carefully and accurately
- Love of interacting with people
- Persistence
- Thorough documentation
- Ability to create a good impression for yourself and your organization
- Ability to help the person you're interviewing understand the benefits for him or her
- Ability to help the person you're interviewing understand what you need from him or her
- Ability to research quickly and thoroughly
- Being able to feel positive very quickly after rejection or an error
- Using a voice that the person you're interviewing interprets as enthusiastic
- Knowing the way the person you're interviewing likes to be communicated with
- Understanding the time limits of the person you're interviewing
- Ability to speak and write effectively—use words that are clear, are concise, put subject and verb first, and use the second person ("you")

Figure 2-1. Successful interviewers' skills

How to Use the Platinum Rule

Applying the Platinum Rule works like magic. To succeed in using it, you need to know three things:

- Your own most comfortable way of communicating
- How to recognize, at a glance, the way another person likes to communicate
- How to modify your own way of communicating to adapt to the other person's way of communicating

By the end of this chapter, you'll know all three essentials for applying the Platinum Rule.

Discover Your Communication Style

Take this highly scientific test that will determine beyond a shadow of a doubt your most comfortable way of communicating. (Really, take it! It will give you insights.)

Communication Style Assessment: Describe the real you by completing the following sentences. Circle only the words that express how you *really* are, not as you would like to be.

I make decisions:	Based on facts	Quickly with details	Based on merit of the idea	After asking others' opinions
I work:	In a controlled manner	At breakneck speed	Very enthusiastically	Steadily/calmly
I am often:	Precisely on time	Rushed	Supposed to be in more than one place	Unrushed
I relate to others by:	Assessing	Commanding	Empathizing	Accepting
I am most interested in:	Facts	Results	Ideas	Building relationships
People often say I am:	Reserved	Dominating	Outgoing	Easygoing
I talk mainly about:	Organizing	Achieving	Goals, ideas, dreams	Personal topics
I respond to others:	Slowly	Impatiently	Animatedly	In a friendly way
When listening I am:	Selective	Impatient	Distractible	Interested
The way I use gestures is:	Rarely	Close to my body	Wide sweeping motions	Openly
My voice is:	Reserved	Direct	Animated	Low-keyed
My work space is:	Super organized	Bare	A disaster	Full of creature comforts
Total circles for each column:	1. _____	2. _____	3. _____	4. _____

Your dominant communication style is the column with the highest number of items circled:

column 1 = Analytical
column 2 = Driver
column 3 = Expressive
column 4 = Amiable

For most people, there will be at least one circle in each column, as each of us is a mixture of styles. For some people, the totals for two or more columns will be relatively close.

So, you're wondering, which style is dominant when the difference is only a few numbers? Is that a split personality? No, it's a relative dominance in two or more styles. That's a great thing, really. It means you're naturally comfortable communicating in more than one way. That makes interviewing a lot easier, since you can more readily modify the way you communicate if there's something comfortable to you in other styles.

OK, so how do you use these four communication styles in interviewing? We'll get to that shortly. First, let's look at how this theory of communicating developed.

How Did the Idea of Communication Styles Develop?

As long as people have been communicating, there have been difficulties because of their differences. And for thousands of years, people have been trying to understand those differences and developing theories to explain them. One such theory that's very valuable for understanding the dynamics of communication has developed over the past 20 years.

Social psychologists David W. Merrill and Roger H. Reid defined our ability to *help each other understand things* as "social style" and described the four styles (Amiable, Analytical, Driver, and Expressive) in detail in *Personal Styles and Effective Performance* (Radnor, PA: Chilton, 1981). We apply the concept of social styles to communication and call it "communication styles" here, because so much of what people do in an interview is to help each other understand what the other is saying.

A few years later, Robert Bolton and Dorothy Grover Bolton focused specifically on *how to modify* to the four social styles in *Social Style/Management Style* (New York: American Management Association, 1984). It's this *ability to modify* that we'll use most to help people give us information in an effective, efficient, and comfortable manner. When you can modify from your most comfortable style to the style of the person you're interviewing, you make it easier for that person to provide the information you want.

> **⚠️ CAUTION!**
>
> ### Get a Second Opinion—at Least
>
> The key to understanding a person's style is *observable behavior*. In doing the Communication Style Assessment, you "observed" yourself. But it's hard to assess yourself accurately. That's why the most accurate way of determining your style is to get someone else to do the assessment.
>
> Merrill developed his theory of the four social styles from his work with insurance companies. He wanted to find out which behaviors successful insurance agents had in common so companies could predict which job applicants would be the best agents. Instead of observing agents in a clinical setting or asking them questions about themselves, Merrill asked his questions of the agents' clients.
>
> So, ask several people with whom you communicate to complete the assessment. Putting their observations together with yours will give you an even better picture of your most comfortable way of communicating.

Two Dimensions, Four Styles

The four styles identified by Merrill and Reid represent how people behave in terms of two dimensions, *assertiveness* and *responsiveness*. Each of us is somewhere between two extremes on an assertiveness continuum and somewhere between two extremes on a responsiveness continuum.

If we combine the two dimensions by crossing the two axes, we get four quadrants, one for each style (Figure 2-2).

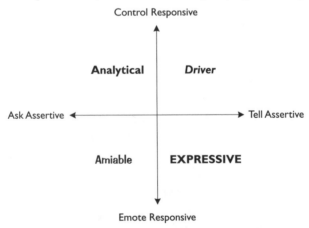

Figure 2-2. The four communication styles

> **Assertiveness** A measure of the degree to which a person influences other people by what he or she says. At one end of the axis is *Tell Assertive*: these people tell what they think. At the other end is *Ask Assertive*: these people ask others' thoughts before telling their own thoughts.
>
> **Responsiveness** A measure of the degree to which a person responds to other people's comments. At one end of the axis is *Control Responsive*: these people use factual, precise words, their body language is reserved, and their facial expressions stay the same no matter the topic. At the other end is *Emote Responsive*: these people convey what they think with facial expressions, colorful words with lots of adjectives, and very open body language.

Now, let's take a few examples to show how we can use this map:

- Abigail says what she believes right away (very Tell Assertive) and her face remains the same no matter what you say to her (extremely Control Responsive).
- Bruce gathers a bit of information before he blurts out his opinions (fairly Tell Assertive) and his faces changes dramatically based on what you say (very Emote Responsive).
- Catherine asks several questions of others before telling her opinions (rather Ask Assertive) and sometimes expresses her reactions to you on her face, but other times you're not sure about her reaction (generally Control Responsive).
- David never tells his ideas until he's asked lots of questions and then checked those answers against other information (extremely Ask Assertive) and his face is always the same no matter the topic (very Control Responsive).
- Elizabeth asks a pointed question before rendering her opinion (slightly more Tell Assertive than not) and tends to use her face and hands carefully, as though she's planned it, when responding to what you've said to her (fairly Control Responsive).

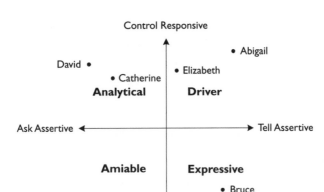

Figure 2-3. Plotting the styles

As you can see, there are degrees of each style. (And you were thinking, "Oh, good! There are only four kinds of people in this world!") People are "all over the map"!

Figures 2-2 and 2-3 also allow us to see the similarities and relationship of each style to the others, so we can see which style will be easier for us to modify to and which styles we have little in common with.

If you're primarily a **Driver**, you'll have to think and plan the most to modify to Amiables; modifying to Analyticals and Expressives will be easier since you have a dimension in common (Control Responsiveness with Analyticals and Tell Assertiveness with Expressives).

If you're primarily an **Expressive**, it will take the most effort to modify to Analyticals; modifying to Drivers and Amiables will be easier because of your similarity (Tell Assertiveness with Drivers and Emote Responsiveness with Amiables).

If you're primarily an **Amiable**, you'll have to work the most to modify to Drivers; it will be easier to modify to Expressives and Analyticals because of the aspects you share (Emote Responsiveness with Expressives and Ask Assertiveness with Analyticals).

If you're primarily an **Analytical**, you'll have to think and plan the most to modify to Expressives; it will take less effort to modify to Amiables and Drivers since you share a dimension (Ask Assertiveness with Amiables and Control Responsiveness with Drivers).

Recognizing Communication Styles and Modifying to Adapt

The key to "knowing" the person you're interviewing is to be able to recognize, quickly, how the person you're talking with communicates and then know how to modify to make him or her feel more comfortable!

If you're an Expressive or a Driver, you're thinking, "I already have the bullet-point highlights needed to recognize the other person's style"—the Communication Style Assessment: it lists the characteristics of each style in a couple words. If your style is Amiable or Analytical, on the other hand, you're looking for lots more information! So here's more for the Amiables and Analyticals—and it's listed in way that's quick and easy for the Expressives and the Drivers.

Recognizing Drivers

Drivers focus on one thing at a time and talk about one point at a time. (They can talk about more than one thing, but it feels disorganized and it's uncomfortable to them.) Some call it "tunnel vision."

Drivers make and use schedules, agendas, to-do lists. They work from the top of the list to the bottom. (If you give them the list of questions for the interview, they'll expect you to ask them in order and since you won't be doing so—see Chapter 3 on using questions—it's best to give them an agenda of the main topic areas.)

Drivers think in the immediate present.

Drivers use primarily nouns and verbs—"job is," "product does," "you need," "get this," "it's done," and so forth. Because of this,

Drivers can appear rude, hard, cold, or even impatient or angry. (But they're not rude, just being quick in their communication.)

Drivers rarely speak about personal things like weather, family, or even the standard pleasantries—"Good morning. How are you doing?" They get right to the point of the interview. (At the end of the interview, they may be a bit more "chatty" since they've accomplished the purpose of the interview.)

Drivers will respond to what you say to them immediately, most times well before there's enough information to know what you're looking for or for them to make a good decision.

The workspaces of Drivers are all cleared off, sterile. It looks like no one works there.

Modifying to Drivers

To communicate successfully with someone who is primarily the Driver style, you need to know what number they're on in their "to-do list" and talk about only that now! I'm being a bit facetious here, but it really will be hard for them to listen if what you want to discuss isn't on their radar screen. It's not realistic that we'll know what the person we're interviewing is thinking about and, even if we did know, we probably need to talk about something else.

Start the interview with the objective of the interview (see Chapter 4 on setting objectives and Chapter 6 on stating them), instead of pleasantries like "Hi, how are you?" Then state how long you'll be together and give a one-sentence description of how you and the other person will work though the interview. This allows the Driver to turn off what they're thinking about and turn on to you. Stick to the time. Even better, send this information ahead of time in writing so they're prepared.

- Drivers like info in writing, because it's likely to be more to the point than verbal (no "chitchat"). Use bold and bullet points instead of sentences and paragraphs.
- Prepare ahead of time so you can be short and concise, to the point.

- Be on time.
- Be energetic and fast-paced. Keep your posture erect. Maintain direct eye contact.
- Start the interview with the objective and get right into the questions.
- Be specific, clear, and brief. Avoid overexplaining, rambling, or being disorganized in any way.
- Focus on results.
- Select the key facts and present them logically and quickly.
- Provide a limited number of options and give them up front.
- Provide quick, concise data (in writing is best) about the pluses and minuses of the options.
- Stay on the topic and keep the pace up.
- If appropriate, ask immediately for a decision.

Recognizing Expressives

Expressives start most sentences with something like "I have a great idea."

Expressives are totally committed to all the "great ideas." (People have a hard time believing this because Expressives jump from thought to thought in interviews. While talking about the first great idea, a second great idea pops in their head and they move on to that one even though they haven't finished expressing the first.)

Expressives appear to never finish anything or any topic.

Since Expressives are happy to jump from thought to thought, they welcome your ideas.

Expressives tend to use language that some would consider exaggerated—lots of adjectives and adverbs, "a lot," "none," "horrendous," "fabulous," and so forth.

Expressives make wide arm movements.

Expressives welcome your participation in their thinking or problem-solving process.

The workspaces of Expressives are full of stuff, with every vertical and horizontal space covered, because they're working on more than one thing at a time and they're very visual.

Modifying to Expressives

To communicate successfully with someone who is primarily the Expressive style, the first thing you need to say (in a really energetic, fast-paced way) is "I have a great idea: let's get started talking about ..." and then jump right into it. Whenever the Expressive gets so excited about something he or she spends more time on it than you need to, use the objective and the agenda to bring the interview back on track.

- Be energetic and fast-paced.
- Keep your posture erect, but not stiff. Maintain direct eye contact.
- Allow time for talking about experiences, opinions, and people. Tell about yourself, too.
- Expressives like debate. They may become dogmatic, but you should avoid doing the same.
- Discover their dreams and goals.
- In support of your ideas, use testimonials from people they like or see as prominent.
- Focus first on the "big picture." Follow up with action plans and concise details.
- Tap their competitive spirit.
- Find a way to have fun while achieving the objective of the interview.
- Keep a balance between flowing with them and getting back on track. (It helps if you comment on the time.)
- Paraphrase what they agree to do.
- Ensure that action plans are made and followed. (It helps to put something in writing.)
- Written things are best when you also use pictures, graphs, charts, and other visuals.

Recognizing Amiables

Amiables use descriptive sentences with adjectives, although not the "exaggerated" wording of Expressives.

Amiables speak very calmly, slowly.

Amiables ask lots of questions about what other people think or how they did things.

Amiables take a long time making a decision because every decision that's made impacts a lot of other people. (In a job interview, expect them to ask you if it's OK if they talk with their friend or spouse or ask to talk with current employees.)

Amiables will always start with "How are you?" If you don't start the interview this way, they'll feel and/or look uncomfortable.

The faces of Amiables are very expressive: when surprised, for example, their eyes are in their eyebrows before they even realize it.

Amiables have a hard time saying no and they take on too much because of this trait.

The workspaces of Amiables have pictures of family, desk drawers with bandages and aspirin and cookies and soup, things in neat piles, and comfortable chairs for sitting and talking.

Modifying to Amiables

To communicate successfully with someone who is primarily the Amiable style, start the interview with their name and "How are you?"—and then listen genuinely to their answer. (See Chapter 7 on listening behaviors.) They'll ask you too and you need to answer genuinely. (If you're a Driver, this feels like such a waste of time!) It's crucial to build a relationship with an Amiable as you start the interview or it'll be difficult to achieve the objective (what you need to know from the interview and how you want the person to feel after the interview). You don't need a half hour of what you might call "chitchat," but simply a brief and sincere exchange to start a comfortable interview.

- Be relaxed and proceed at a moderate pace.
- Lean back somewhat.
- Speak in a moderate volume. Avoid harshness.
- Be genuine.

- Invite their comments by drawing out their opinions and then listening reflectively (instead of judging their ideas and countering them with logic).
- Encourage the Amiable to express any doubts or misgivings.
- Facilitate decision making by telling them what others have done or think and getting them to agree on a deadline for letting you know their decision.
- Mutually agree on goals (probably initiated by you) and action plans with completion dates.
- Offer your support and follow through on your responsibilities.

Recognizing Analyticals

Analyticals use precise, specific words and facts, figures, reason, and logic.

Analyticals like lots of information—all the information!

Analyticals make decisions after they gather all info known to man, woman, child, dog, cat, and guppy in the universe—and then analyze that info. They want to make the perfect decision; this takes time.

Analyticals have a hard time with things that are new or changes. (Why change? They researched and analyzed and made the perfect decision, so why do they need a change or something new?)

Analyticals ask you for lots of information—what, where, when, why, how, who.

Analyticals rarely speak about personal things like weather or family and rarely even exchange the standard pleasantries—"Good morning."

Analyticals speak deliberately, obviously choosing their words carefully.

Analyticals appear calm in any interview. Their faces most of the time look like they're concentrating. (That's because they're always analyzing something.)

Analyticals think in the past—"How did this affect that?" etc.

Analyticals rarely show outward enthusiasm (smiling, laughing, saying, "That's great"). If they like something, it may be hard to tell. (If they say, "That's good," it's likely to be the highest compliment they give.)

Modifying to Analyticals

To be successful communicating with someone who is primarily the Analytical style, start the interview by stating the objective of the interview (instead of "Hi, how are you?" and so forth) and then indicating how long you'll be together, followed by a one-sentence description of how you and they will work though the interview. Then describe the process in detail. Absolutely send a written description ahead of the interview when possible. If it's not possible, at least provide one for them to follow when they walk in the door.

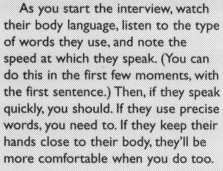

If in Doubt ...
What if you're not sure what style someone is?
   As you start the interview, watch their body language, listen to the type of words they use, and note the speed at which they speak. (You can do this in the first few moments, with the first sentence.) Then, if they speak quickly, you should. If they use precise words, you need to. If they keep their hands close to their body, they'll be more comfortable when you do too.

- Give them information in writing, so they can then sit alone and analyze the information.
- Be on time.
- Speak at a moderate pace. Avoid using a loud voice.
- Get to the questions quickly.
- Be prepared, systematic, factual, logical, and exact.
- List the pros and cons and all the alternatives.
- If you propose or promote an idea or a decision, show why what you think is best and that there's relatively little

risk. Avoid exaggerating the advantages, as Analyticals are turned off by overstatement.

- When possible, allow them to proceed deliberately, even slowly.
- Follow up in writing.
- Set interim dates and ending dates, along with a progress update, in order to meet deadlines.
- End the interview on time but graciously.

Practice, Practice, Practice

Now you know the essential characteristics of Drivers, Expressives, Amiables, and Analyticals. Can you recognize them? The box below, "You Can Recognize the Styles!" lists a dozen phrases we've all heard. For each phrase, identify which communication style would use it.

You Can Recognize the Styles!

Choose the communication style you believe would be most likely to say each of the following:

Mistakes are the portals of discovery. _____

Pick battles big enough to matter, small enough to win. _____

Victory belongs to the most persevering. _____

Patience creates confidence and a rational outlook that leads to success. _____

Which part of "no" don't you understand? _____

I'm talking and I can't shut up! _____

Young at heart, slightly older in other places. _____

The secret of staying young is to find an age and stick to it.
_____

People who think they know everything are very annoying to those of us who do. _____

I look 30, act 20, feel like 60, I must be 40. _____

If you don't like my attitude, call 1-800-WHO-CARES? _____

I'm unreliable, irresponsible, immature, undisciplined, inefficient, disorganized, and inconsistent, but I'm fun. _____

Now, for the answers, look on the next page.

To create enough comfort for the person you're interviewing to give you information easily, it's crucial to recognize the per-

You Can Recognize the Styles! (Answers)

Mistakes are the portals of discovery. **Expressive**

(Expressives talk and do before they think, so they make more mistakes than others. But this doesn't bother them—as it would bother Drivers, who see mistakes as a waste of time—because Expressives see mistakes as giving them more ideas.)

Pick battles big enough to matter, small enough to win. **Driver**

(Drivers want to be right, but they won't waste time with things that don't matter.)

Victory belongs to the most persevering. **Analytical**

(Analyticals are like the Energizer Bunny®: they just keep going and going. They know that if they keep asking questions, keep looking for info, they'll be able to make the perfect decision.)

Patience creates confidence and a rational outlook that leads to success. **Analytical or Amiable**

(Both Analyticals and Amiables seem patient because of the time they take to ask questions, listen to the answers, and give ideas)

Which part of "no" don't you understand? **Driver**

(Drivers state their idea or decision and don't understand when anyone treats it as if it were open to question.)

I'm talking and I can't shut up! **Expressive**

(Do you really need an explanation here?)

Young at heart, slightly older in other places. **Amiable**

(Only Amiables could look so positively and so calmly on the aging process. You can imagine the calm voice, the smile on their face, the serene facial expression as they say this.)

The secret of staying young is to find an age and stick to it. **Analytical**

(Analyticals don't like change. Once you've asked all the questions and gotten all that info and analyzed it all and made the one perfect decision, why would you change?)

People who think they know everything are very annoying to those of us who do. **Driver or Analytical**

(Both Drivers and Analyticals get impatient with people without facts—interesting since the Drivers move so fast they often don't have facts themselves.)

I look 30, act 20, feel like 60, I must be 40. **Analytical**

(Only Analyticals would think in this logical progression.)

If you don't like my attitude, call 1-800-WHO-CARES? **Driver**
(Drivers are very matter of fact, and it appears to us that they don't seem to care how we think or feel.)

I'm unreliable, irresponsible, immature, undisciplined, inefficient, disorganized, and inconsistent, but I'm fun. **Expressive**
(This is how people think of Expressives, becase their sentences have numerous thoughts and they jump from topic to topic.)

Styles and Strategies

Nine months into her new position as Associate Director of Libraries for Public Service at a major state university, Suzanne Adkins realized that something was not right. Not the position itself—Adkins enjoyed planning, research, helping other staff learn their jobs, and the many other responsibilities. She particularly enjoyed the opportunities to affect, in innovative ways, the growth and development of her department. She felt that her active and successful leadership as a manager would someday lead her to direct a major university library.

The position was fine. The problem was the Director: Suzanne couldn't get information from her or even give it in a way that created action.

Here's just one example. A few months after she started the position, Suzanne made an appointment to meet with the Director to get feedback on a strategic plan for a new outreach and instructional program. She had carefully detailed the plan: it specified resource needs, space arrangements, departmental assignments, staff schedules, and publicity. She and her staff were anxious to implement the plan as soon as possible because it promised to be challenging and they wanted to be well under way by the next semester.

Suzanne started by giving the Director the detailed written plan and then began to present the various parts. Her plan was to present it all, then ask a few questions about areas for which she knew the Director would provide great input. About halfway through the presentation, the Director interrupted, indicating that she would read through the plan carefully and get back to Suzanne soon. She then changed the conversation to another subject.

Three months later, Suzanne had heard nothing, so she reminded the Director of their conversation. The director appeared somewhat disturbed and indicated she would respond as soon as she had time to read and approve the prepared plan.

What style is Suzanne Adkins?
What style is the Director?
What should Suzanne have done to get the information, feedback, and eventually agreement she needed from her boss?
What should the Director have done to get what she needed from the interview?
Now, turn the page to compare your answers.

son's style and then modify your behavior and words. This is like any other skill: with practice, you'll be doing this with less thought than you may need now.

The scenario, "Styles and Strategies," gives you an opportunity to identify the styles of an employee and her boss and to suggest ways in which each could modify her behavior.

Caution: Contents Under Pressure!

Have you ever seen someone behave very uncharacteristically, using a different communication style? That change in styles may surprise us, but we can prepare for it. That's because every communication style has a predictable *backup style*.

Backup Style

The backup style emerges naturally when a person is under excessive stress (such as during a job interview or a performance appraisal) or angry (such as with a customer with a problem). When we feel more stress than we're comfortable with, we react unconsciously: the fight-or-flight response leads us to exaggerate our strengths, to go to extremes, the better to act on our response. For people who are more *Tell Assertive* (Drivers and Expressives), the response is generally *fight*. For people who are more *Ask Assertive* (Analyticals and Amiables), the response is generally *flight*.

Thus we can expect the following changes in style:

- *Drivers* act even more like "it's my way or the highway."
- *Expressives* are extra enthusiastic, but usually in a negative and/or attacking way.

Styles and Strategies (Answers)

What style is Suzanne Adkins? **Analytical**

(She enjoyed planning and research. Her plan was carefully detailed.)

What style is the Director? **Driver**

(She interrupted Suzanne halfway through: Drivers don't like long descriptions and are even more irritated when the information is all written out. She hadn't read the plan after three months: it was far too detailed for a Driver, so she put it aside.)

What should Suzanne have done to get the information, feedback, and eventually agreement she needed from her boss?

First, she should have asked the Director how she wanted the information. In writing? If so, what should the plan include? In an oral presentation? If so, what should it cover? In writing and orally?

It's likely her director would have asked for a written list: just the facts—using phrases, not sentences. If she wanted to meet, it would be only to ask Suzanne questions, not to hear it all again.

Then, Suzanne should have asked the Director for a deadline for the written list and a date by which she could expect a decision on the plan, telling how her plan would save time, money, and other resources. (Drivers are motivated to take action by time and other efficiencies.)

What should the Director have done to get what she needed from the interview?

The Director should have told Suzanne that she wanted a written list of the main points of the plan and she should have given her a written example of the type of information and the format she expected.

Then the Director needed to listen to Suzanne's many clarification questions and answer them. When the descriptions got longer than she needed, she should have paraphrased them so Suzanne would know the Director understood.

Finally, she should have agreed on a deadline for Suzanne to submit her plan and a date for asking Suzanne questions so the Director could make a decision.

- *Amiables* acquiesce even more than usual ("Oh, it's no problem, it's fine"—even though you were late for the appointment and now they'll be late for their next appointment).

- *Analyticals* withdraw even further from making statements or decisions.

This backup style provides immediate relief of stress for the person—and immediate stress for you the interviewer. This, as you can imagine, quickly puts an end to the feeling of relief. Thus, to keep the interview as comfortable as possible, you need to recognize that the tension has caused the person to switch to his or her backup style and you need to minimize your reactions of discomfort while getting the person back on track.

Secondary Backup Style

If the person can't get relief from stress or tension, he or she will move into their *secondary backup style.* The secondary backup style, as people get progressively more uncomfortable, results in behavior that's opposite the primary style:

- *Drivers* acquiesce.
- *Expressives* avoid.
- *Amiables* say, "My way or the highway."
- *Analyticals* attack.

Imagine, then, how these people will feel later.

You definitely want to prevent any circumstances that might result in feelings of regret or worse. Help the person you're interviewing reduce tension by taking a break, by faking a coughing fit and leaving the room—anything to give him or her a few minutes of space alone to recover. Reschedule if necessary.

Avoiding Stress and Backup Styles

It can be disconcerting when backup styles emerge. In fact, they can easily ruin an interview. That troubling prospect should be one more compelling reason to prepare for each interview, to plan ways to modify your communication style so the other person feels more comfortable—and so you're less likely to be facing backup styles.

Planning to Modify Your Way of Communicating

If you know anything about the person you'll be interviewing, it will help to plan a strategy by filling out the Communication Style Strategy Sheet (Figure 2-4) before the interview, so you can keep in mind how the other person communicates and how he or she will expect you to communicate. Use the Communication Style Expectations Tool (Figure 2-5) to help you fill out the strategy sheet.

What if you don't know the person at all? Use the Communication Style Expectations Tool during the interview to identify the person's dominant style and to help you to modify to it. It should take only a few moments to identify the style and then you can anticipate what he or she will be expecting from you.

Now you're thinking, "But I do all my interviewing face to face. I can't keep looking at a piece of paper while we're talking!" Ah, the beauty of paper forms—they all look alike to the person facing you. Since you'll be using other paper-based interview tools (see Chapter 4 on creating and using interview tools), the person you're interviewing won't even know that

Observable Behavior	Name		
Priorities			
Pace			
Problem Solving			
Decision Making			
When They're Upset, They (Backup style)			
Measure Their Value By			
What I'll Do to Modify			

Figure 2-4. Communication Style Strategy Sheet

Observable Behavior	Driver	Expressive	Amiable	Analytical
Priorities	Get things done	Tell others ideas, plans, dreams	Keep everyone happy	Make correct decisions/ perfection
Pace	Quick	Quick	Calm	Deliberate
Problem Solving	Fast with few details (dislikes problems)	Fast with few details (loves it)	Slowly with lots of details about how it will affect others	Slowly with lots of question asking and time for analysis
Decision Making	Fast with few details	Fast with few details	Slow with lots of details about how others have done it	Slow with lots of information and time
When They're Upset They (Backup style)	Speak in very clipped sentences, loudly, no room for another's ideas	Speak loudly, quickly; exaggerate, talk on and on	Acquiesce to whatever anyone says or stop talking/ refuse to answer	Acquiesce to others' ideas
Measure Their Value by	Getting things done their way	Applause/pats on the back	Attention	Activity
Let Them Save	Time	Effort	Relationships	Face
Needs a Climate That	Allows them to build their own structure	Inspires them	Suggests ideas	Provides details
Take Time to Be	Efficient	Stimulating	Agreeable	Thorough and accurate
Support Their	Conclusions	Dreams and intuitions	Feelings	Principles
Give Benefits That Answer	What	How	Who	Why
For Decisions, Give Them	Options and probabilities	Incentives	Guarantees and assurance	Evidence

Figure 2-5. Communication Style Expectations Tool

you're using the Communications Style Expectations Tool.

Planning to Gain Information from People Who Are Different from You

The title of this section probably should have a subtitle—"The Effects of Experiences, Attitudes, Beliefs, and Values"—because we're all different. So, let's face it: anybody that you interview will be different from you. You don't need me to tell you that— and you would need many, many books to cover this topic properly. Here are few tips to help you.

The Essentials of Successful Interviews

Successful interviewers:
- Realize that success in interviewing depends on applying the Platinum Rule—"Do unto others as *they* would have you do unto them."
- Know their own communication style.
- Recognize Driver, Expressive, Analytical, and Amiable communication styles.
- Are able to adapt their communication style to connect better with others.

Recognizing the communication style of the person you're interviewing and modifying to it will help you connect with him or her. When we modify, we're communicating in a similar way, which makes it easier for the person to understand us, to feel comfortable, and thus to give us information we need. It's all about making a connection!

So, imagine that you're doing an interview right now. There you are (being the incredible communication style recognizer and modifier you are now), modifying like a pro to a Driver—using short, right-to-the-point sentences, looking directly at the person, talking quickly .... But the person is sitting in cold silence.

What's happening? Did you miss something? Is he really not a Driver?

Look again. He may well be a Driver, but you need to go beyond that.

In addition to recognizing his communication style, you also needed to find out about his experiences, attitudes, beliefs, and values. It just so happens that the person you're interviewing comes from a culture in which looking directly at someone is aggressive and talking business before inquiring about each other's health and general well-being is impolite. The person's experiences, attitudes, beliefs, and values are influencing how he understands what you're communicating.

We've been focusing on communication style because a person's style underlies all of his or her communication. But on top of style are all of the experiences, attitudes, beliefs, and values that each of us brings to any situation. When you communicate with somebody, your perception of what the other person is communicating becomes what you understand him or her to mean.

Perception refers to how we see the world, other people, and ourselves. It's very personal and it's powerfully influenced by our "filters." Two people in the same situation, receiving the same words, facial expressions, body language, and voice can have very different perceptions of what it all means. Each processes the message through his or her filters—experiences, attitudes about the topic or the person or people like the person, and beliefs and values from his or her culture and family. Becoming aware of filters and attuned to them—yours and the other person's—is vital to successful communication. Ignoring the powerful influence of filters in communication results in increased misunderstandings and frustration, making it more difficult to gain information in an interview.

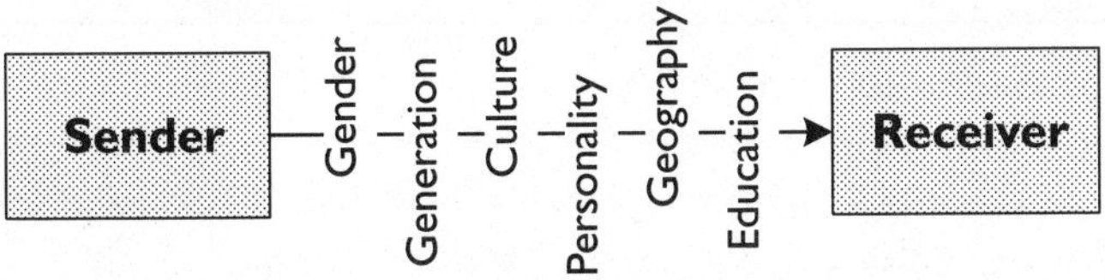

Figure 2-6. Perception filters (transforming the message between sender and receiver)

There are two reasons why any of us might ignore someone's filters.

A belief that one's own attitudes, beliefs, and values are the best. People of either gender, of any generation, culture, or personality, or from any geographical location or educational background can believe that their own attitudes, beliefs, and values are the best. Within this mental context, a person may dismiss any information about different values, practices, and attitudes as wrong or defective. In some settings, this reaction may come out in such forms as racial slurs, sexual harassment, or true ethnocentrism. In a polite business setting, however, it will come out as talking down to the person—which makes it harder to create comfort and thus gain information.

TRICKS OF THE TRADE

Perspective Shift

In the absence of books or people to help you learn:

Think of someone whose differences are hard for you to understand. Think about the things that are different about that person. Now shift your point of view. (You might find it helpful to actually get up and sit in another chair to face the one you just left.) Imagine that you are in the person's body and mind. You now see yourself from the *center of his or her universe*. As if you were that other person, answer these two questions. What are you thinking about *you*? What would you like *you* to do differently to help you understand and feel comfortable?

You can do this during an interview as well (although you should refrain from changing chairs!), to keep focused on communicating in ways the other person will understand and feel comfortable with.

Not knowing enough about filters to recognize them.
Sometimes when we communicate, we're simply doing what comes naturally, without realizing that the people around us are different in significant ways. If that's your situation, get specific information from excellent books about the effects on communication of gender and generational, cultural, and other differences. I'd recommend *Mars and Venus in the Workplace: A Practical Guide for Improving Communication and Getting Results at Work* by John Gray (New York: HarperCollins, 2001) and *Voices of Diversity: Real People Talk About Problems and Solutions in a Workplace Where Everyone Is Not Alike* by Renee Blank and Sandra Slipp (New York: AMACOM, 1994). You can also talk with people you know who are different from you and ask them to tell you about their attitudes, beliefs, and values. Remember that what you learn from a book will be general and what you learn from a person may be very individual. But what you learn and the sensitivity that you develop will help keep you aware that we all communicate differently.

Some qualities make it easier to gain information from people who have different experiences, attitudes, beliefs, and values:

- **Respect**—All people desire respect. To communicate successfully with people who are different from you, avoid stereotyping and ethnocentrism. Remember that you're communicating with a person, not a culture or a gender or a belief. Respect involves showing consideration for people's individual needs.

- **Awareness**—Knowledge of another person's background facilitates understanding. It also reduces communication errors, which you may be unaware of committing. Developing general awareness will make it easier to notice individual differences in an interview.
- **Empathy**—Try to see things from the perspective of the other person. Empathy allows you to understand and still disagree with the reasons for someone's feelings or actions in a situation. It also requires you to acknowledge what the other person's reasons are.
- **Interest**—Becoming genuinely interested in learning about another person's experiences, attitudes, beliefs, and values can foster goodwill and improve communication. Get the conversation started by telling about yourself. (Avoid personal issues such as age, family information, religion, and so on.)
- **Flexibility**—These kinds of differences cause added stress in interview situations, making it difficult to gain the information we need. Avoid communication breakdowns by remaining flexible. You were planning to ask questions in a certain way or have the person write something or meet other people and you discover you need to change your plan—a bit stressful for you, but do it. Remaining rigid ("my way or the highway") will only increase frustration and add to your stress.

Manager's Checklist for Chapter 2

❑ In every interview, there are at least two parties, the sender and the receiver. It is always, always, always the sender's job to make sure the receiver gets the information the way he or she needs it in order to take in the information easily and understand it.

❏ The Platinum Rule is "Do unto others as *they* would have you do unto them." To do so, you must know:

- Your own most comfortable way of communicating
- How to recognize, at a glance, the way the other person likes to communicate
- How to modify your style to the other person's style

❏ Determine your communication style—Driver, Expressive, Analytical, or Amiable. Use the Communication Style Assessment and then ask several other people to assess you. Combining the assessment results will give you a more accurate picture of your most comfortable way of communicating.

❏ Each communication style has a predictable backup style. It emerges when the person is under excessive stress or angry.

❏ Plan for each interview by using the Communication Style Strategy Sheet and the Communication Style Expectations Tool.

❏ Use the strategy sheet and the expectations tool during the interview, along with your other interview tools.

❏ Be alert and attentive to the other person's experiences, attitudes, beliefs, and values and modify your communication so he or she has an easy time understanding and feeling comfortable.

What Questions Should I Ask—and How?

A window of opportunity won't open itself.
—Dave Weinbaum

The right questions, asked in ways that make it easy for the person to answer completely, will reveal the information you need. The right questions in behavioral interviewing are always based on the objectives—what you need to know from the interview and how you want the person to feel after the interview. We'll be working on how to determine those objectives for each interview in Chapter 4 and how to get them across to the person you're interviewing in Chapter 6. In this chapter we'll focus on the questions.

What Types of Questions Should You Ask?

Your job is to ask questions that elicit a response that provides the information that meets your objectives. There are two basic types of questions: closed and open-ended.

A *closed* (or *closed-ended*) question elicits a yes or a no or other one-word responses:

> **Key Term**
>
> **Question** An interrogative expression used to elicit information. That's how your dictionary might define this word. Here we're using it in a broader sense, as any expression (interrogative or declarative) used to elicit information. The word "question" comes to us from Latin, where it derived from the verb *quaerere*, which meant either to ask or simply to seek.
>
> **Closed (closed-ended) question** A question that elicits a yes or a no or other one-word responses.
>
> **Open-ended question** A question that elicits responses of any type and length.

- What is your name?
- Have you finished the report?
- What's the cost of your product?

An *open-ended* (or *open*) question elicits responses of any type and length:

- What qualifies you for this position?
- How can I help you with the report?
- Why is your product suitable for our needs?

We'll get to each of these types of questions in a moment and discuss advantages, disadvantages, and strategies. But first, we need to briefly discuss two qualities that are essential to a successful interview—*variety* and *fluidity*.

Variety

For most interviews, you'll need a mix of types of questions to keep the person interested, which allows for a feeling of easy conversation instead a choppy question-answer, question-answer feeling.

You've been through those types of interviews with interviewers who are less experienced:

Interviewer: Do you have a plan of action?
You: Yes.
Interviewer: When will you finish implementing it?
You: Friday.
Interviewer: Will it work?

You: Yes.
Interviewer: Do you need my help?
You: No.
Interviewer: When will I see a report?
You: Monday.
Interviewer: Will I need to take any action?
You: Uh-uh.
Interviewer: ....

Are you bored yet? Are you really able to pay attention anymore? Are you already doing something else and so not paying attention? You can see how close to impossible it is for the interviewer to get from you the information needed with this type of questioning. The interviewer is putting you to sleep. He or she is not engaging you because the interview is not conversational. The interviewer is using only one type of question—closed.

It's easy to believe, then, that all we have to do to avoid the deadly question-answer, question-answer interview is use mostly questions that get people to talk—open-ended. But you can have interviews that are just as boring, choppy, and non-conversational with open-ended questions.

Here's a perfect example. The interviewer asks you a question. You answer with descriptions and examples. Then the interviewer asks you the next question on his or her list, which has nothing to do with what you were just saying. There's no transition, no comment on your answer, just the next question—and then another and another and pretty soon your descriptions are getting shorter and shorter.

It's not the *type* of question that makes the interview succeed or fail. It's the *mix* of the types of questions!

Fluidity

Another quality that's essential to a successful interview is fluidity. A good interview flows smoothly, naturally.

How fluid are your interviews? Check your "fluidity index": think about a few people from whom you've tried to gain information and mark each of the seven statements as true or false.

		Your Fluidity Index
True	False	
❏	❏	1. I don't like my interview to run too long, so I always keep a tight rein on the conversation.
❏	❏	2. I purposely ask general questions so I'll get lots of information. I believe if you ask very specific questions, the person will answer only those and then you'll get less information.
❏	❏	3. I permit no interruptions when I speak.
❏	❏	4. I prefer the person I'm interviewing to be businesslike and brief.
❏	❏	5. I have a list of questions to ask and I ask the questions in the order on my sheet, waiting for the person to answer each before I ask the next question. If the person accidentally gives me answers to a question I haven't asked yet, I always ask it when I come to it anyway—better to be sure I've covered everything.
❏	❏	6. I encourage small talk about the weather.
❏	❏	7. I don't hesitate to strike off in an unexpected conversational direction, even though it uses time and it may not lead to any information directly related to the objective of the interview.

Scoring: *Give yourself 10 points each for checking 1, 2, 3, 4, and 5 False and 6 and 7 True.*

If you missed any of the items, the following might help:

1, 3, and 4—There is great value in structuring the interview and keeping it businesslike, since it's is important to both of the parties to use the timer efficiently. However, when that structure comes across as strict and doesn't allow for interruptions, there will not be a conversational flow. So you'll be on time, but you won't have achieved either of your objectives.

2—Wanting to get as much information as possible is great and it sure seems like you'd get more if you asked very general questions ("Name all the tasks you don't like"). Actually, what happens when you ask general questions is that the person has to spend some time figuring out exactly what you mean and/or constructing such a long list. Asking more specific questions ("Name the tasks in your last job that you didn't like") gets you faster, more accurate and thorough answers. The person has an immediate picture of what you want so it's easier to answer. When it's easy for someone to come up with the information, it's likely to be more accurate. (In Chapter 8, we'll deal with the person who's intentionally avoiding the truth.)

5—Having a list of questions is great. However, you need to be flexible with the list. As you do, the interview will be more conversational and the person won't be irritated by questions asking for information that he or she has already given.

6 and 7—For an HR professional like me, saying it's a good thing to encourage small talk is a frightening prospect. In employment interviewing, I do everything to avoid the legal issues surrounding a person giving me information that's not specifically related to the skills and characteristics required for the job. (More on this in Chapter 5, "Legal Issues.") For every type of interview, a allowing a little time for "off the topic" conversations will create comfort, increase the conversational feeling, and give you information you didn't even realize the person had. This is true for employment interviewing as well, but there you need to be really careful to keep the topics to weather and traffic! As soon as you ask candidates about their holiday or weekend, you risk hearing about their family or church—information that you're likely to not need. (Hold on—I'll explain in Chapter 5.)

If your score is below 50, here are some quick suggestions:

- If you use the same list of questions for repeated interviews, make changes to the questions from time to time.
- Write the objectives for the interview at the top of the list of questions, for a visual reminder of what you want to accomplish. This will help those of us who tend to be more direct. Remember to reach your objectives, you need a conversational feeling to keep the information flowing.
- Be prepared to ask questions based on what the person says, even if the questions are further down on your list

or not on your list at all. This may be to get more information from your earlier question—probing—or because
what the person says naturally leads to another area
you'd planned to cover.
* Practice the skills in this chapter!

Fact-Finding Questions—Closed Questions

Closed (or closed-ended) questions have gotten a bad rap in
the past as questions that elicit only a "yes" or "no" or short
factual answer and therefore don't encourage the person to talk.
But closed questions are best in certain situations.

If you need certain pieces of information (like names, dates,
and serial numbers), you can get them most efficiently with
closed questions. Sometimes it's crucial to get only the information you need and nothing else. For example, if you're interviewing a job candidate and you need to know if there would be
any obstacles to meeting requirements for attendance and
punctuality, asking if the candidate has a family or is involved in
other activities will get you information you don't need to have.
(In fact, such inquiries create a legal liability, as we'll discuss in
Chapter 5.)

There are also times when closed questions are best
because you need to be very careful not to lead the person to
the answer, such as if you're interviewing customers in focus
groups to find out about any potential needs.

Your goal should always be to get the information you need
and make it easy for the
person you're interviewing
to give it to you. So in
addition to varying the
types of questions you
ask, vary the way you ask
them. There are several
ways to ask closed ques-
tions:

> **TRICKS OF THE TRADE**
>
> ### Closed Questions
>
> Use closed questions in the
> following situations:
> * You're seeking specific information.
> * You're touching on a topic where
>   the person could tell you things you
>   don't need to know—or things it's
>   risky to know.
> * You need to be very careful not to
>   lead the person to any answer.

With a question mark—Your voice rises at the end of the sentence, marking it clearly as a question. Example: "Are formal meetings your best way to communicate?"

Without a question mark—The structure and intonation indicate a statement, which makes this way of eliciting information especially useful with someone who's upset. Example: "Tell me if formal meetings are your best way to communicate."

Multiple-choice—You give alternatives from which to pick, when you need to focus the person. Limit the choices to three or it will be hard for him or her to remember. Example: "I'm going to name three methods of communication. Pick the one that you feel is the way you best communicate—formal meetings, written communication, or one on one, face to face?"

Ranking—You ask the person to rank choices, when you want to find out what's important to him or her but you don't need a full discourse or when you need to focus the person. You can then follow up by asking an open-ended question to understand the reasons behind the ranking. Limit the choices to three or it will be hard for him or her to remember. Example: "I'm going to give you a list of three methods of communicating. Tell me your first choice, your second choice, and your third choice—formal meetings, written communication, and one on one, face to face."

Binary—You ask the person to pick from two opposite terms, when you need information about how strongly he or she feels about something but you don't need a full discourse or when you need to focus the person. You can then ask an open-ended question to understand why he or she chose the one term over the other. Example: "Which better describes the way you like to communicate—formal meetings or off-the-cuff?"

When you ask a closed question (with question mark or without), you'll normally use the words "when," "where," or "who" in your question or it will consist of a statement, either inverted or in normal order introduced by "if" or "whether" (e.g., "Are you making progress with this project?" or "Please tell me whether you're making progress with this project"). For multiple-choice, ranking, and binary questions, you'll use such phrases as "Pick the one" or "Which one of the following ...?" You'll never use the words "how" or "why" in a closed question.

Questions, Questions, Questions

You're interviewing a potential customer to find out whether the person needs the products or services of your organization. Write a closed question of each kind to elicit the information you need.

with question mark:

without question mark:

multiple-choice:

ranking:

binary:

   Now, check your questions against the descriptions and examples above.

Get-Them-Talking Questions—Open-Ended Questions

An open-ended question—one that uses "how" or "why" or words like "describe," "list," "tell me about"—is incredibly effective at getting a person to give you more than one-word answers. However, an open-ended question will often cause a person to pause (often for a long time), to shift around uneasily, to look down or away, and finally provide a tentative 10-word answer—unless the question you ask has to do with past or current behavior.

   To make it easy for the person to give you the information you need, use *only* behavioral open-ended questions. Since this book is based on the belief that behavioral interviewing is the way to meet your objectives—to gain the information you need and make the person feel like you want him or her to feel after the interview—why do I hit you over the head paragraph after paragraph, chapter after chapter, with the terminology?

Because old habits die hard and new habits take some time to form and stick.

You're working on improving your interviewing skills. If you hear and see and practice something often enough, it'll become second nature. (And when you're in the room with the person, you won't be able to say, "Oh, hold on a minute!" and go get this book to look up how to construct a question!)

Good Questions, Bad Questions	
Behavioral Open-Ended Questions	**Hypothetical Open-Ended Questions**
• Describe a time when you needed to say what you thought, even though it made you unpopular with your coworkers.	• Describe what you would do if you disagreed with the way one of your coworkers was handling a situation.
• Tell me where you are on each of the Action Plan items.	• Some people have trouble getting all their Action Plan items done. Why do you think that is?
• Why haven't molds released in the past?	• Why do you think the mold isn't releasing?
• Describe a situation in which you were able to get all your filing done (even if it happened only once).	• Imagine you were able to create the exact service you needed to get all your filing done. Describe exactly how it would look.
• List the things your product will do for us.	• Tell us about the things that make other customers happy with your product.

Just as with closed questions, behavioral open-ended questions can be asked with a question mark or without. Remember that with a person who is upset in any way (nervous, angry, pressed for time), it's better to go without a question mark. The statement tone ("Describe how you created that spreadsheet") is less likely to add to the negative feeling than the rising inflection of a question mark ("How did you create that spreadsheet?").

Questions to Follow up on Responses or Comments

Here's the real magic to creating that conversational feeling in an interview. During the interview, no matter how perfectly

TRICKS OF THE TRADE

Open-Ended Questions

Use open-ended questions in the following situations:
- You want to get ideas, examples, and more complete answers.
- You've asked more than two closed questions in a row and you want to avoid a "choppy" feeling, to keep the interview more conversational so the person gives you complete information.

Questions, Questions, Questions

You're preparing to interview each of your direct employees. Write a behavioral open-ended question of each kind that will help you discover what methods they will use to achieve one of their performance appraisal goals, to submit their completed monthly report to you by the last day of the month.

with a question mark:

without a question mark:

Now, check your questions. Are they open-ended? Is there a difference in inflection? Are they based on past or current behavior?

you've constructed your questions, the person is going to give you information that isn't quite specific enough for you to be sure you understand what he or she means. How useful is the information conveyed by such answers as these?

- I'm really trustworthy.
- I really liked that product.
- I'll be finished at the end of the week.

To get information you can use, you're going to need to ask one or more clarifying questions. So, what are the best types of questions to ask in these situations?

With the first two examples above, you need a description of what the person means, so you'll follow up with an open-ended behavioral question. The reason is obvious: you're asking the person to clarify something. If your question isn't behavioral, the person may pause, shift around uncomfortably, and try to figure out what you want. All you want is clarification without making the person feel incompetent for not being more specific! Ask the question using some of the words the person used, such as "Describe a time you were really trustworthy" or "List the specific things the product did that you really liked."

With the third example, you simply need a day and a time, so your follow-up question will be closed without a question mark. You phrase your question as a statement because that makes it less likely that the person will perceive it negatively.

Let me explain. A clarifying question indicates that the answer wasn't sufficiently clear. The person may take your follow-up question as a judgment of his or her ability to communicate. In this situation, a question with a rising inflection may seem like an accusation. (That's especially likely if you're even slightly irritated about needing clarification, since the rise will be even greater.) In addition, closed questions tend to be shorter and therefore may sound clipped or curt to someone sensitive to the need to clarify. Also, it's difficult to start a closed question without a bit of punch and a frown ("What do you mean by 'the end of the week'? Friday afternoon?"). So we can create discomfort at the beginning and the end of the question!

That's why it would be best to follow up with a closed question without a question mark. For the third example, you'd say, "I need to know what day and time you'll be finished this week."

Questions to follow up on responses and comments are not questions you can write in your Interview Planning and Conducting Tool (hang on; we'll develop this in Chapter 5) ahead of time. However, it'll be easier to come up with the questions "on your feet" when you have a formula for creating them. In asking clarifying questions, restate some of their words in the form of a question. If the response or

> **Follow-up Questions** Tricks of the Trade
>
> Use follow-up questions in the following situations:
> - The response is incomplete or not specific enough for you to understand.
> - You don't understand what the person said.
> - You believe the person is avoiding telling part or all of the information or even avoiding telling the truth.

Clarifying Can Cause Leading

CAUTION!

When you ask clarifying questions, avoid questions that suggest an answer in the way you word them. Here are some examples of clarifying questions that lead.

The person you're interviewing says:

"In my last job I was in sales for 10 years. The company sold equipment cleaning services to various industries."

→ "I suppose you enjoyed working in sales, didn't you?"

"Karen hasn't turned in her reports in Word for three months and we've had several talks about this type of rule breaking."

→ "You didn't let her get away with breaking the rules, did you?"

"There are several choices for ways we can meet production increases, including opening up a new plant in Mexico."

→ "Would you agree that next year we ought to open a plant in Mexico?"

"The third tray for 11x17 paper is way more expensive than any of the other features you mentioned. The last time we talked I gave you my budget information and it hasn't changed."

→ "I guess you don't want that feature because it costs more than you budgeted."

"As new customers sign on for our services, we gather lots of information and we document it all."

→ "You probably do the same as we do: gather the information and then document it on a form."

What to Do to Avoid Leading

One way to avoid asking leading questions is to avoid certain words and phrases, such as "I suppose," "I guess," "probably," "would you agree," "you didn't," "maybe," "hopefully," "wouldn't you," "couldn't you," "shouldn't you," "didn't you," "did you." All of these words and phrases suggest an answer.

Instead, start with words and phrases like "Describe," "List," "Tell me," and "I need to know."

So, for example, if the person says, "I don't want that feature," you'd ask, "I need to know what about the feature makes it not fit your need."

comment is long or complex, you should reduce it.

Of course, while you're asking questions in response to their comments, you're interacting, not just asking question after question. This creates much more of a conversational

---

Write a Clarifying Question

Write a question that will help the person you're interviewing clarify what he or she meant by "I think we should increase our production this year." (Use the examples above to guide you. Avoid using any of the words that can cause leading questions.)

Is your question an open-ended question without a question mark? That's generally the best way to follow up when you need more information.

---

flow. Ah! Here's a way to make for an *automatic* conversational feeling!

How to Decide What Questions You'll Ask

The order in which you ask the questions and the behaviorally oriented structure of the question itself will affect the conversational quality of the interview. A great tool to help you create questions that will lead you to the objectives (gain the information you need and make the person feel the way you want him or her to feel) is the STAR Behaviors Process.

This process comes from the Targeted Selection (for employment) process created by Development Dimensions International, Inc. (DDI), which developed it originally for use during the interview. DDI suggests that during the employment interview the interviewer listen to the answers provided by the candidate with an ear toward Situations/Tasks, Actions, and Results (STAR). This helps the employment interviewer listen for the behavioral information he or she needs about the applicant's past behaviors and future potential. (In Chapter 5, we'll discuss using STAR during all kinds of interviews.)

We'll use STAR here to help us write questions before the interview that are behavioral and focus on the specific information we need to gain. A behavioral question (a complete STAR) will lead the person you're interviewing to give you information on the *situations* he or she was in or *tasks* he or she did that surrounded the *actions* he or she took that finally led to *results*. Sometimes one question will give you all the information you

STAR Behaviors Process A process developed by Development Dimensions International, Inc. (DDI) for use during employment interviews. The process focuses the interviewer on the answers provided by the candidate in terms of Situations/Tasks, Actions, and Results (STAR).

need in each of these areas. Other times, because of the complexity of the information or because of the person's communication abilities, you'll need a question for each of the three parts of STAR. Planning ahead with a question in each of the three areas puts you in the best place for gaining the information you need. Of course, you want to mix the types of questions as well. Be prepared to *not* ask all the questions you've developed. Keep that conversational quality going by asking only the questions necessary to get the information you need!

Focus on Objectives Don't let preparation distract you from purpose. It's likely won't need to ask all of the questions you've prepared. Remember: your objective is not to ask questions but to *gain information*.

The STAR Behavioral Questions Worksheet shows a situation and the four questions to use to get information about *situations/tasks*, *actions*, and *results*.

Now make your own example.

First, check the box next to the person you're interviewing for this example:

❏ candidate for employment or volunteer work
❏ direct employee
❏ peer
❏ current or potential customer
❏ vendors, other managers

Second, write the information you need to gain (the reason for the interview):

Third, write at least two questions in each of the three STAR

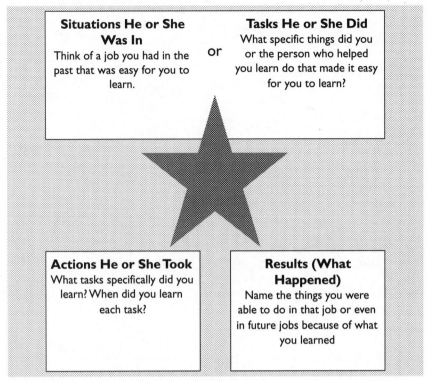

Figure 3-1. STAR Behavioral Questions Worksheet

areas that will help you gain the information you need to gain. Make your questions behavioral: ask about past or current behavior ("Describe a time you were really trustworthy" or "When did you receive the call?"). Use a mix of the types of questions:

- Closed with a question mark
- Closed without a question mark
- Multiple-choice
- Ranking
- Binary
- Open-ended with a question mark
- Open-ended without a question mark

(Refer to the section "What Type of Questions Should You

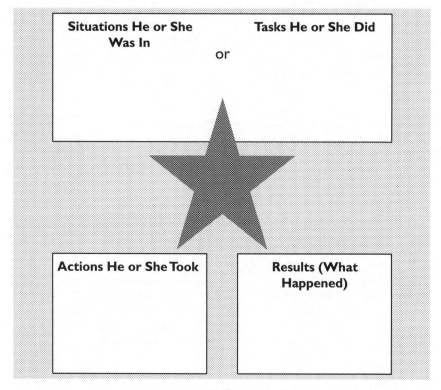

Ask" earlier in this chapter for more details about creating types of questions.)

We'll work a lot more with the STAR behavioral interview questions as part of the Interview Planning and Conducting Tool in Chapter 5.

How Should You Ask the Questions?

We send messages with our facial expressions, body movements, tone of voice, emphasis, and pauses as well as with the words we use—whether others understand those messages as we mean them or not. The people we're interviewing receive our message through all of their senses and then they understand it through the following:

- their communication style (Chapter 2)

- their attitudes, beliefs, values, and experiences (Chapter 2)
- their relationship with you
- their attention and stress levels at the time

These things can easily cause them to change the meaning we intended to convey in our message.

Consequently, we need to prepare to ask the questions in a way the person we're interviewing is most likely to understand them. That means we need to know about the things listed above for the person we're interviewing. Some of those things we may not be able to find out in advance because we don't know who the person is, so we'll have to "think on our feet."

We already have ideas for recognizing and modifying to their communication style and ideas for asking questions of people in terms of their experiences, attitudes, beliefs, and values. As for the third point listed, if you don't know the person, you know that his or her relationship to you is new!—and that usually creates some initial discomfort that you can be prepared to alleviate. (We'll discuss this in Chapter 6). Finally, you'll regularly have to watch for attention and stress level during the interview: it's not just about the person or your relationship with that person or even the situation, but also about the day and the time.

Whether or not you can plan in advance for each person and each interview using our Interview Plan, you can understand about the various aspects involved when you ask questions:

- your facial expressions
- your gestures and posture
- the tone and volume of your voice
- how and where you pause or not
- the words you emphasize with tone, volume, and pauses
- your words

Two things you know only too well from experience:

- Facial expressions, gestures and posture, tone, volume, pauses, and/or emphasis can contradict the words you choose. For example, a quick frown says something negative even while you're simply asking, "How much do you know about chemistry?"

- When the two are contradictory, the person will take the meaning from the physical aspects rather than from the words. For example, if you fold your arms while saying, "Describe your role on the ABC project," you're telling the person that you're expecting a response that is less than truthful or that isn't going to impress you. He or she hears your words, of course, but your face and body and voice speak louder.

Since the person you're interviewing will be using your face and body to interpret your questions, we'll spend most of our time on the most successful ways to use them to achieve your objectives. (In Chapter 9, when we discuss technology, we'll consider ways to work more on your voice and wording choices when the other person can't see your body.) All of the ideas below are broad generalizations and a great place to start.

We've already discussed some specifics in Chapter 2, in terms of modifying to people with different communi-

---

Test the Whole Package

Smart Managing As you write questions, think about what facial expression, posture and gestures, tone, volume, and pauses you'll use. Be alert for questions that are likely to cause you to send contradictory messages.

Test your questions, if possible. Ask a colleague or a friend to play the part of the person you're going to interview, in the interview location. Ask your questions and then request feedback. Did the other person understand your questions as you intended them? If not, why not?

When you find a potential problem, try one of these two suggestions:

- Change the wording of the question to fit what's going to happen naturally to your face, voice, and body.
- Write "stage directions"—"pause," "keep face calm," etc.—next to each question.

	Driver	Expressive	Amiable	Analytical
Face/Body	OK to have longer than usual eye contact, resting face, few gestures	OK to have longer than usual eye contact; excited face, smiling when appropriate; wide, sweeping, fast gestures	Shorter than usual eye contact; smiling when appropriate; calm face; gestures are slow but many	Shorter than usual eye contact; resting face; few gestures
Voice	Fast paced; pause only for extreme emphasis; a bit louder than normal	Fast paced; no pauses; very positive, upbeat; a bit louder than normal	Slower than usual; pause for emphasis frequently; calm and caring; a bit softer than normal	Slower with careful enunciation; pause for emphasis frequently; calm and in control; normal volume
Words	Nouns and verbs, few and to the point, verb first	Lots of adjectives and verbs; to the point; positive	Lots of adjectives and adverbs; many words descriptive of people	Factual, measurable, specific; many words
Words (specifically for clarifying questions)	Start with: "We'll be able to save time if I knew ..."	Start with: "What a great idea! Tell me more about ..."	Start with: "It would help me a lot if I knew..."	Start with: "I know how important having all the information is to you. I'd like to know ..."

Figure 3-1. How to ask questions to fit the other person's communication style

cation styles, with suggestions for asking questions of Drivers, Expressives, Amiables, and Analyticals. Figure 3-1 provides suggestions for face, body, voice, and words. Also in Chapter 2, we discussed interviewing people who are different from us, primarily in terms of experiences, attitudes, beliefs, and values.

Face

Use a smiling or a "resting face" (no expression other than direct eye contact) for *most of the questions* you'll ask and with *most of the people* you'll be interviewing. People around the world recognize the facial expressions that accompany the emotions of happiness (smile), fear or uncertainty (little eye contact), anger (clenched teeth, pursed lips, severe/deep frown), and surprise (quickly raised eyebrows, open mouth). These expressions are understood universally, across cultures.

The eyes, the "windows to the soul," can tell their own story. Maintain eye contact for *five to 10 seconds* before looking away, to communicate involvement with the other person. It's most natural, so it makes people in one-on-one or group situations (like focus groups) most comfortable so they'll have the easiest time answering your questions.

More is not better in this case: eye contact for more than 10 seconds communicates intimacy or intimidation—and it's unlikely you'll want to communicate *either* intimacy or intimidation in any of the questions with any of the people in any interview. On the other hand, extremely brief or intermittent eye contact may make the other person feel that you're not sincerely interested in a conversation or that you're nervous. Here's the major place where we'll see difference between cultures: many North Americans want eye contact during conversation, while people of other cultures find such direct eye contact discomforting or even a sign of disrespect.

Body

Gestures made with any part of the body can speak volumes. At their *best*:

- They add emphasis.
- They illustrate.
- They help the other person visualize.
- They create rapport.
- They match the words.

At their *worst*:

- They're distracting.
- They create confusion when they don't match the words.
- They reveal your nervous energy.
- They make you appear unauthentic or less than capable.

For example, you may blush in embarrassment, shrug to indicate that you don't know something, tilt your head or furrow your brow to communicate that you don't understand, give a hand signal that conveys your approval, fold your arms in front of you to suggest that you have your own ideas, or tilt your head up to show contempt. Some gestures mean different things for people from different cultures.

In general, when asking questions you'll create comfort and consistency of meaning for most people when you *use your hands to illustrate your words.* When you're asking a multiple-choice question and you say, "three choices," hold up three fingers, for example, or when you're saying, "Describe all the experiences you've had with ...," spread your hands about the width of your body when you say the word "all."

Avoid the following:

- Pointing at the person.
- Making jerky movements.
- Playing with anything (your pen, your clothes, objects on your desk or the table, etc.).
- Repeating a gesture many times.

Lean toward the person while you're asking the question to show interest in the answer. Your posture can also reveal your status or level of confidence. Imagine how you would respond to a person with slumped shoulders and a shuffling walk. How differently would you respond if that same person had a straight back and a quick pace?

Voice

The tone of your voice, the volume, the pace, and your use of pauses also carry more of the meaning of your questions than your words. The most effective *tone* is *positive.* The most effective *volume* will generally be *even throughout* the interview. *Vary the pace* depending on your words—*faster* for descriptions of *events* (to convey excitement about actions) and *slower* when you're asking for descriptions of *problems* or for *information* about the person (to show the person that what he or she says about a problem or about himself or herself is really important to you).

Pausing and emphasizing certain words by using a different tone of voice is incredible for drawing attention to specific parts of your question, especially if it's long.

Say each question below several times. Each time emphasize a different word and pause in a different place.

- "Who did you work with on that project?"
- "I have three choices of ways for you to learn WordPerfect ...."
- "Tell me about the great idea you have for next year's planning process."
- "What difficulties are you having with this product?"
- "Describe a previous project in which you needed to be available 24 hours a day."

Wow! There are so many places to pause and words to emphasize in each question—creating many different meanings.

And that's only for emphasizing and pausing. When you add all the possibilities for your face, your body, your tone, your volume, your pace, and your words, it's no wonder that a question that seems so straightforward to us as we ask it can cause such different reactions and bring us such different information!

The greater your ability to intentionally create and control meanings when you ask questions, the more successful you'll be at interviewing. Knowing about the effects of facial expressions, gestures and postures, tone of voice, emphasis, pauses, and wording choices will not only help you construct the questions for your Interview Planning and Conducting Tool (which we'll do in Chapter 5), but will also allow you to better construct questions on the spot to follow up on a response to an earlier question.

Manager's Checklist for Chapter 3

❏ Use only behavioral questions, ones that ask about past or current behavior, to help the person you're interviewing provide specific information related directly to what you need to know.

❏ Create a conversational quality by mixing the types of questions, skipping questions for which you've already received an answer, and using some of their words to ask clarifying questions.

❏ Use your face, body, tone of voice, volume, pacing, pauses, and emphasis as well as word choice to make sure the other person understands what you mean.

❏ Use what you know about modifying to other communication styles when you construct questions and choose the ways in which you'll ask them.

How Should I Plan for the Interview?

One must step back in order to take a better leap.

Planning needs to begin long before the person you're interviewing arrives—and even before you set up the interview! "But," you say, "I don't have time to plan and I'm good at winging it." Well, since you're reading this chapter, I believe I have a shot at convincing you.

Planning is as much for the benefit of the person you're interviewing as for you. What planning does for *the other person*:

- It saves time during the interview.
- When there's evidence we planned, the person feels like we want to do this, we have time, and it's important.
- Since the person knows what will happen in the interview, he or she feels more confident and more prepared to give us the information.

What planning does for *you*:

- It saves time during the interview.
- It reduces nervousness.
- It reduces mistakes.
- It allows you to get the information you need, especially in situations where it may be difficult to get accurate information (e.g., with direct-report employees in performance appraisals or other performance situations, with customers who have a problem with your service or product, with peers who differ with you on an approach, a plan, the direction of a project, etc.).

Planning takes time, of course, but it's smarter to invest time in avoiding mistakes than to spend it fixing mistakes and/or talking your way out of them. You can avoid mistakes by creating a comfortable atmosphere with the variety of behavioral, easy-to-answer questions that create a conversational feel. You can avoid mistakes by asking those questions using the communication style of the other person. You can avoid mistakes by following an agenda that you gave to the person in advance, so he or she knew what to expect. You can avoid mistakes by gathering information ahead of time so you know what you need to gain from interviewing the person, as opposed to what you could gain from others or in writing.

Remember, you have two objectives: to gain specific information (the *information* objective) and to make the person feel a certain way about you and/or your organization after the interview (the *feeling* objective). Proper planning will help you achieve your information objective and get you started on the right path for achieving your feeling objective.

Let's face it: no matter how great you are at recognizing and modifying to people's communication styles and coming up with questions as you go, without planning and preparing you won't have sent the person anything in advance and you won't have interview tools. These are visual first impressions that you've planned for the interview, making the person feel welcome and comfortable.

Setting Objectives

Would you get on a bus if you didn't know where it was going? I did one summer, when I was traveling for two weeks just to go places. But even my "no objective" bus trip had an objective: "to go places." It may not have been specific, but it was an objective.

Even when we think an activity has no objective or we don't need an objective to motivate us or to help us get where we're going in the most efficient, accurate way, there's always an objective. Humans take action for a reason, for a purpose, to meet an objective.

You think you didn't set an objective for the last interview you did? Maybe not in the way we're discussing here, but how did you know when the interview was over? You looked at the clock and the 30 minutes had passed that you usually allow (objective) or you felt the problem was solved (objective) or you decided then and there that the candidate wasn't right for the job (objective). Without planning formally, you set objectives anyway.

Since you're going to set objectives, why not do it a little more formally and gain the incredible benefits of speed, efficiency, and accuracy that a specific, planned objective can gain for you and the person you're interviewing? (Very few of the people you need to interview will be willing to get on that bus without knowing where it's going. They're busy people, not college students having fun for two weeks at the end of the summer!)

We set objectives so we can plan to achieve them. We set

Information and Feeling Objectives

When the interview is over, I'll know what words and tone of voice my staff person used when talking with Mrs. Jones on the phone Thursday. I'll also know what action he took after the call to resolve the problem.

When the interview is over, my staff person will know what Mrs. Jones said she felt because of what was communicated and what she'd like to do next to resolve the problem she called about. He will understand that I'm ready to discuss ideas for how he'll resolve this and that he has my support throughout the process.

objectives so others who'll be involved in achieving them can know where they're going, how to prepare, and what to bring. The objectives tell us all what the end looks like.

A SMART, written objective is the foundation for a successful interview:

Specific
Measurable
Attained
Realistic
Time-based

Your objectives need to be so **S**pecific that even anyone who isn't knowledgeable about the situation can understand what it means. When objectives are that specific, there's never a concern that the other person didn't understand the words you chose or what you meant.

Your objective also needs to be **M**easurable, so that there's no doubt whether you've achieved it or not. An objective that's measurable is also of greatest value when you plan. If it isn't measurable, you'll know it isn't specific enough for the other person to have the same understanding as you do.

Write the objective as though it were already **A**ttained. Which objective do you find more motivating to you?

"Learn what other companies in your industry the vendor works with, how much time their service will take, and how much it will cost, by the end of the interview."

OR

"Know what other companies in your industry the vendor works with, how much time their service will take, and how much it will cost, by the end of the interview."

Most people will find the second objective more motivating. "Learn" is a process, while "know" is a result. A process implies effort, while a result implies completion, success. So, expressing an objective as attained is more motivating, just as when athletes visualize their success.

Your objective needs to be **R**ealistic: you need to be able to achieve it with this person, in the time available or allotted, and it needs to be meaningful given the reason for the interview. "Why even mention 'realistic'?" you might be wondering. "Of course my objectives will be realistic. Who would plan something *un*realistic?" But this criterion makes you think about your perception of what's "realistic" and ask the following questions: "Can the person I'm planning to interview help me achieve this objective? What time will I need to achieve this objective? Is this objective appropriate for this type of interview?"

Your objective needs to include a **T**ime—"by the end of the interview." That's easy enough!

When an objective is written before the interview and it's SMART:

- You can use it in planning for the interview.
- You can let the person you're interviewing know it ahead of time so he or she can prepare.
- You'll be able to express the objective to the person in the interview easily, without reading from your interview tools.
- You'll be able to make changes as the interview progresses and not go off track, because you'll know it so well.

The format of the objective is up to you. After you write it, read it to be sure that it meets each of the five SMART criteria.

> "Know what other companies in your industry the vendor works with, how much time their service will take, and how much it will cost, by the end of the interview."
> *Know* = **A**ttained
> *what other companies in your industry the vendor works with, how much time their service will take, and how much it will cost* = **S**pecific and **M**easurable
> *by the end of the interview* = **T**ime
> **R**ealistic: it's realistic to believe that a vendor who knew the objective in advance would be able to provide you with this information.

Figure 4-1. A SMART objective

Are These Objectives SMART?

Indicate for each objective whether or not it meets the SMART criteria (yes or no).

	Specific and Measurable	Attained	Realistic	Time
1. Know what the customer wants.				
2. Gain information about the needs of all project team members by the end of the meeting.				
3. By the date agreed upon after the interview, candidate will call with any clarifying questions about the teller position discussed.				
4. Consultant felt they had our full attention during the entire interview.				
5. Have written objectives, completion dates, and action steps.				

(For the answers, turn the page.)

You'll get the opportunity to rewrite these objectives as SMART when we work on the information objectives and the feeling objectives in the next sections.

What Do You Need to Know from the Interview?

Here's where you create information objectives, writing exactly what information you need to gain from the interview. Your objectives will allow you to plan the questions and other methods you'll use to gain the information. You'll also communicate these objectives to the person you're interviewing, in writing or verbally, in advance of the interview and then state these objectives verbally at the beginning of the interview.

The number of objectives depends on the person and the purpose of the interview. You may have written interviewing objectives before reading this book, but they probably were less

	Specific and Measurable	Attained	Realistic	Time
1. Know what the customer wants.	No	Yes	No way to know without knowing the person. In 1, 2, and 5 we don't have specific enough information about the topic. In 1 and 5 we need to know the time.	No
2. Gain information about the needs of all project team members by the end of the meeting.	No	No		Yes
3. By the date agreed upon after the interview, candidate will call with any clarifying questions about the teller position discussed.	Yes	No		Yes
4. Consultant felt they had our full attention during the entire interview.	Yes	Yes		Yes
5. Have written objectives, completion dates, and action steps.	No	Yes		No

Are these objectives SMART? (Answers)

specific than we're promoting here. When you make your objectives specific, you'll usually have more, since you'll be listing many things you need to know, not just writing a global

MISTAKE PROOFING

What Do You Mean Specifically?

Is your objective specific enough? Here's a suggestion to check it: restate your objective as an "if" question.

Let's assume, for example, that your objective is "Have given the consultants all the information about our company."

Ask yourself (and answer, of course!) this question: "If I'd given the consultants *all the information about our company*, what would I have given them?"

Your answer might be "the organization chart, the marketing brochure, ..." These are the specifics that need to be in your objective(s). (You didn't really mean "all" or you would need at least a wheelbarrow to deliver *all* the information!)

Just imagine if you asked an assistant to gather "all the information" on your company, would he or she understand exactly what you wanted—no more and no less? Be specific!

objective, such as "Ask questions relating to the job to know if the person is the best candidate."

Make 'Em SMART!

Rewrite these not-yet-SMART objectives from page 73. Hint #1: Look back to the answers to see how the objectives weren't SMART. Hint #2: Use the suggestion in the sidebar, "What Do You Mean *Specifically?"*

1. Know what the customer wants.

2. Gain information about the needs of all project team members by the end of the meeting.

3. By the date agreed upon after the interview, candidate will call with any clarifying questions about the teller position discussed.

4. Have written objectives, completion dates, and action steps.

(For the answers, turn to page 77.)

Now that you've rewritten some sample objectives, try to write some from scratch. It's likely that you have an interview coming up. So, use that interview as the basis for going through the items in "Create Information Objectives."

Create Information Objectives

Who are you interviewing (potential candidate, direct employee, peer, customer, vendor) and why (employment, volunteer, performance appraisal, development plan, project plan, focus group, problem solving, discovering buying needs, assess for services to your organization)?

List all the things you'll need to know in order to make a hiring decision or the things you'll have done during the in-person performance appraisal interview or what information you'll have after the focus group or what information you'll have after the sales appointment in order to develop a proposal, etc. (continued on next page)

> •   •
> •   •
> •   •
> Use the list above to write as many SMART information objectives as
> you need.
> •
> •
> •
> •
> •
> •
> Is each of your objectives SMART? Underline and mark the parts of
> each objective that satisfy the five criteria—**S**mart, **M**easurable,
> **A**ttained, **R**ealistic, and **T**ime.

Now you're ready to start planning the rest of the interview
so it helps you achieve these objectives and then to communicate the objectives to the person you'll be interviewing.

How Do You Want the Person to Feel After the Interview?

In most interviews we don't communicate the feeling objective.
It mainly functions as a guide in planning the methods to
achieve the information objectives and to keep us on course
during the interview. Remember: the person is going to feel
something in the interview. You should be directing that feeling!

> **Feeling Objectives**
> By the end of the interview, the customer feels the compa-
> ny is working on their problem fast enough to have it fixed
> by Friday.
> By the end of the interview, the candidate feels positive enough to
> tell others about openings for employment even if she's discovered
> this position doesn't fit her skills and interests.
> By the end of the interview, the consultant feels he gave thorough
> enough information that we'll be able to make an informed decision
> whether to use his services.

Make 'Em SMART! (Answers)

Here are examples of ways to rewrite the not-yet-SMART objectives:

1. Know what the customer wants.
   Know what the customer's choices are from the service menu by the end of the interview.

2. Gain information about the needs of all project team members by the end of the meeting.
   Have a list of what information each project team member needs in order to begin their piece of the project by the end of the meeting.

3. By the date agreed upon after the interview, candidate will call with any clarifying questions about the teller position discussed.
   By the date agreed upon after the interview, candidate has called to ask any clarifying questions about the teller position discussed.

4. Have written objectives, completion dates, and action steps.
   Have written objectives, completion dates, and action steps for this year's personal development plan that are agreed upon by employee and manager by one week after the interview.

Create Feeling Objectives

Use the same interview "who" and "why" as shown in the box "Create Information Objectives," and the information objectives that resulted. Write all the things you want the person to feel.

-
-
-

-
-
-

Use the list above to write one SMART feeling objective. (Write two, if there are really two distinct feelings that you want to direct.)

-
-

Is your objective SMART? Underline and mark the parts of each objective that satisfy the five criteria—**S**mart, **M**easurable, **A**ttained, **R**ealistic, and **T**ime.

We then use the feeling objective as we're determining the methods we'll use to gain the information and as we're setting the environment for the interview.

For example, if we want the person to feel we're working fast enough for the problem to be fixed by Friday, one of the methods we'll use to gain information is to start with a really brief account of another customer whose problem was fixed quickly. This will give the picture that we have experience in fixing problems, which will make the person more open to giving us information, feeling that it will lead to a quick resolution. We'll also plan to gain whatever information we need during the interview (rather than having the person fill out forms later or look things up and call us back) and quickly and concisely.

Determining and Setting the Environment

A person comes to an interview expecting that you'll have set the environment. This is part of preparing properly, to arrange a reception appropriate to the situation, so as to make the person feel comfortable and start the interview on the right foot.

There are only two exceptions.

The first exception is when the interview is unplanned, as when a direct employee has a performance issue that you must deal with as it's happening or when a vendor drops in or a customer calls with a problem to be solved. In these situations the person can feel like you're prepared if you at least have a place where the two of you can sit and talk. Leave him or her

TRICKS OF THE TRADE

Prepare for the Unexpected

Even in situations for which you can't plan, you can plan. Use the Environment Checklist to keep a space generally prepared. If the space in which you do most of your interviewing is your workspace, this will be relatively easy. It takes a bit more orchestrating if you do most of your interviewing in a conference room used by others for other purposes or a variety of conference rooms depending on availability.

Enlist others to help. Show them your checklist and explain the benefit to them, that leaving the room ready for interviews will help them achieve their own objectives. The other ways in which the room is used are likely to include gaining information and making people feel a certain way, so by helping you they're benefiting themselves.

where you met (assuming it's moderately comfortable) and then, when you've found the place and turned on the lights, etc., you'll be able to lead the person to a space that's "ready."

The second exception is when it would actually increase the person's comfort by letting him or her have some control in setting the environment. This might be the case, for example, when you're working with a peer to solve a problem. You create that comfort from your relationship and from your past behavior that conveyed the suggestion, "Make yourself at home." So when the person comes into your space, he or she might feel more comfortable moving the chair, creating a space on the side of your desk for his or her papers, getting candy out of the dish, bringing a drink, or whatever. Another situation in which the other person might comfortably participate in setting the environment is when you're interviewing a vendor or a customer in his or her workspace.

Use the Environment Checklist to determine what preparations you need to make to set the environment. There are some things you'll check off for every person and in every interview situation (a clean room with chairs and a place to write, your materials, handouts). What you check off and what you plan will differ slightly or dramatically from person to person and certainly in different interviewing situations. For example, you need more space and furniture for a focus group of customers than to meet with a peer to come up with a solution to a problem.

Environment Checklist

Interview Objectives:

I'll need this environment to meet these objectives:
• Date and Time (actual interview time start/end)
• People Involved (names, relationship to the reason for interview)

• Furniture and Seat Who Where (draw furniture and people in relationship to each other)

- Room (make room free from materials that will distract because they aren't part of this interview)

AV Equipment and Audiovisuals Checklist

AV Equpment
- ❏ flipchart paper/easel
- ❏ LCD projector/computer
- ❏ screen
- ❏ audiotape player
- ❏ video and monitor
- ❏ computer w/-w/o Internet access access
- ❏ telephone
- ❏ audio/video conference

Audiovisuals
- ❏ prepared flip charts
- ❏ posters
- ❏ transparencies w/frames
- ❏ screen show or other files loaded and CD/disks of the files
- ❏ audiotape (queued and ready)
- ❏ videotape (queued and ready)
- ❏ all equipment tested and ready to use

Handouts Checklist
- ❏ agenda
- ❏ organization marketing materials
- ❏ job description
- ❏ employee handbook
- ❏ forms or surveys to complete
- ❏ specs for project
- ❏ customer order info
- ❏ other, depending on reason for interview

Supplies Checklist
- ❏ pads of paper (with or without organization logo)
- ❏ pens, pencils (with or without organization logo)
- ❏ blank cassette tapes
- ❏ videotapes
- ❏ CDs
- ❏ flipchart markers
- ❏ highlighters
- ❏ Other:

Your Materials Checklist

❑ All your interview tools (completed Environment Checklist,
Interview Planning and Conducting Tool, Communication Styles
Expectations Tool, Communication Styles Strategy Sheet, blank paper)
❑ Refreshments

Distractions to Plan Out Checklist

❑ Telephones/pagers/e-mail ringing for you or others in the interview
❑ People coming in to talk/deliver messages/bring refreshments
❑ People leaving and returning frequently
❑ Bright sunlight
❑ Too hot/too cold
❑ Busy activity visual or audible in hall or through window

Key for Completing the Environment Checklist
Interview Objectives: Rewrite your information and feeling
objectives, to have them handy while determining and setting
the environment. Remember to choose only those items that
will help you meet your objectives.

Date and Time: Decide how much time you need you need to
gain the information at a pace that won't make anyone feel
bored, rushed, or anxious about the time. Then choose a day
and a time that are most appropriate for the interview. (For
example, if you schedule a performance appraisal at the end of
the last workday of the week, even the most dedicated employee will likely be less focused than at another time.) Do your best
to schedule the interview for a time and day when the person is
at his or her best. (If that timing would be terrible for you, com-
promise.) If it's impossible to schedule at a best time, you can
at least prepare for what you'll need to do for yourself or for the
other person to make the most comfortable environment.
Choose a day and a time that are typically the least busy, so
you're least likely to be delayed in starting, to get distracted,
and to have problems if you need to be flexible.

People Involved: Pay special attention when the interview
includes more than you and one other person, such as with

focus groups of customers, vendors who may bring a colleague, job interviews involving a team, or project and planning meetings with several employees. Decide who needs to be involved and the maximum and minimum for the objective. Then look at how those people are related and how comfortable they'll be together, so you can plan the rest of your environment to help you achieve your objectives.

Furniture and Seat Who Where: Have enough chairs. Avoid chairs with wheels (so people don't roll away from you or show their nervousness as they roll and/or rock). Instead, choose solid chairs with wide legs.

Have a table or a desk to write on. Place people so the table or desk creates no interference between you and them, to promote rapport. If it's just you and another person in your workspace, place the chair on the side of your desk. If the two of you are at a conference table, place both chairs at a corner, so the table is not fully between you. If there are several people around a table, you can avoid making it a barrier by being even more careful to not lean on it or pull yourself right up close to it. It's crucial to sit up straight in your chair (so less of your body is behind the table) and use open body language (arms not crossed). (See Chapter 7 for body language.)

When you have more than one person in the interview, where you guide people to sit makes a difference in how easily you'll gain information. You can make the other people feel important if you put them at the heads of a rectangular or oval table, but be sure you're not in the center or you'll soon have a neck ache from turning your head left and right, back and forth, depending on which of the people is speaking. Place yourself where you can see as much of the people's bodies and faces as possible without moving around a lot, so you don't get tired and you don't become a distraction.

Room: Choose a room that's the right size for the number of people. (If it's far too big, create a smaller space by setting up the AV, handouts, and supplies in the corner closest to the door.) Ensure privacy if the interview is with a job candidate or a direct employee. In some interviews with customers, peers, and vendors as well, privacy is important. Always think about the information you'll be gaining as you plan for your privacy needs.

Remove materials that will distract because they aren't part of this interview. Obviously a clean and organized space conveys a more positive image of your organization. If you can't remove irrelevant materials, at least organize them: books and magazines are less distracting on shelves than in piles, for example, and papers are better neatly stacked than scattered about. This is relatively easy if it's a conference room. But if the interview is in your workspace and you're not neat and organized, move the interview to a conference room.

Key for Completing Audiovisuals and A/V Equipment Checklist
Using visuals to supplement your words will help you meet your information objectives by making it easier for the person to understand what you need. It'll also help you meet your feeling objective, since a person who understands easily is much more likely to be comfortable. Test the equipment and queue the materials to start; if you can't use them easily and smoothly, you'll likely make the other person uncomfortable. Use visual equipment that allows you to keep all the lights on. The person will need to read any handouts and to see you—and to stay awake! And you will need to read your interview tools and write in them and to see the person's facial expressions. (There are lots more ideas on AV equipment when used as the medium of the interview in Chapter 9.)

Key for Completing the Handouts Checklist
As described above, handouts will help you gain information. They also provide the other person space for taking notes and a source of information that he or she can take away from the interview.

Key for Completing the Supplies Checklist
If you have all the paper, pens, staplers, etc. you need, you won't have to leave or ask someone to bring something. That will save time and keep the conversational flow.

Key for Completing Your Materials Checklist
These crucial tools help you keep on track and give you a place to write the information you're gaining during the interview. (You need accurate information later for making decisions. None of us will take 30 minutes after every interview to write notes and it's impossible to have accurate information if you can't remember the look on a person's face or even his or her specific words.)

Refreshments: Having water, coffee, tea, juice, cream, sugar, lemon, cups, spoons, and napkins available in or near the interview room makes for a comfortable environment. In some cases, such as with focus groups or group planning meetings, snacks or meals are appropriate. If you choose to include food in your interview, be sure that the arrangements don't distract from the information-gaining process.

Key for Completing the Distractions to Plan Out Checklist
Distractions cause a loss of focus, time, and comfort and make it harder to achieve your feeling and information objectives. They also make you seem less prepared, less caring about the other person and the interview, and less professional. Tell people what you're doing and for how long. Tell them not to disturb you, then specify any exceptions (emergencies, important calls, etc.) and a procedure for notifying you if necessary. Use signs to keep people out of the room. Have someone cover for you if your job or the day and time necessitate a presence. And be sure to turn off any phones and pagers.

There are so many distractions that you can't plan out, but do what you can to "shelter" the interview and make the other person feel valuable.

> **Smart Managing**
>
> **Take Five**
>
> Plan five minutes (more if possible) after the interview to write information in your Interview Planning and Conducting Tool before your next interview or other task. This is time to write things you didn't have time to write at a particular point in the interview. Reserve these five minutes for writing only. Avoid allowing this time to become a cushion in case the interview goes longer than planned.

What if you're in the other person's workspace, as is so often the case in a customer interview? The following experience may offer some insights.

I was interviewing a customer to determine his needs for our services. He was on the phone and stayed there for 15 minutes after I arrived. His office had suit jackets on the backs of all the chairs. The office was filled with smoke. It was very cold and he was wearing a winter coat. There were piles of papers on the floor, on the desks, on the chairs. Most of the surfaces were visibly dirty. (This was the General Manager's office in a posh hotel.)

When he got off the phone, he excused the mess and said it was his temporary office while the new property was being built. (Oh, I felt better until I learned that the building was started two months earlier and had three months to go.) He then moved our interview to the bar. (It was 9 a.m., so no customers would be there.) We had to talk about his need for making some pretty serious changes in the way staff performed, but our conversation was hampered by lack of privacy. You guessed it—the employee with the greatest needs worked in the bar. In addition, the owner of the hotel was there, reading the newspaper. During our interview, his cell phone rang once and he talked on it, the phone in the bar rang and he took that call, and his next appointment came into the room 10 minutes early.

Somehow I got a lot of information—but it still remains to be seen if it's accurate. And I definitely wasn't even in the same universe with my feeling objective and the outcome!

What did I do to set the environment? Nothing—and I beat myself up all the way back to the office for doing nothing! I set objectives, I set an agenda, I communicated it to him ahead of time, I gathered information before the interview, and I wrote a beginning, questions, and an ending. And then, after all that, I skipped the environment, thinking I had no control! I just let the other person set the environment (and he wasn't very good at it).

I knew I was going to a hotel and I know how hotels are laid out physically. I know the potential for distraction and the types of distractions that are likely in the environment and with the type of position he held.

In the future, I'll use my Environment Checklist when planning and preparing for interviewing in someone else's space. I will plan the optimal environment and what I'll do (in general) if we don't have it.

I'll use my ability to modify to people's communication styles as I use words, voice, face, and body that will be comfortable to that person when I request that he turn off his phone for the next 30 minutes or not smoke during the interview or that we meet somewhere without staff or owners. No matter what his communication style, I'll emphasize the benefits to him for doing these things.

For example, I should have said, "We can create more specific solutions for your staff performance issues if it's just you and I. Let's move to the table I saw in the blue room."

I could have helped set a better environment. I'm looking forward to my next interview in someone else's space so I can practice.

The little details matter in setting the environment. In fact, it's likely to be the littlest detail that's the most important in helping you reach your objective—or in creating the disaster interview that will show up as an example in a seminar or a book on interviewing!

We are all so busy we zip through the world not noticing things that are business as usual. When you take care to make the interview environments different—by arranging a suitable space, by minimizing distractions, by providing appropriate handouts and other takeaways—the people that you interview notice and you create the comfortable environments that put the people at ease and make them aware that they're valuable.

Determining and Setting the Plan: Agenda and Methods

Start with a general agenda and then modify the order of the beginning based on the person's communication style and the reason you're interviewing. (See Chapter 6, pp. 109-111.) If you know the person you're interviewing, you can make the modifications now in your planning. If you don't know him or her well enough to be sure, you can identify the communication style in the first few moments and then quickly change the order of the beginning so your First Communication fits that style. Having a written agenda and planned beginning allows you to simply draw arrows and off you go.

General Agenda
Beginning:
  First Communication
  Our information objectives
  The other person's objectives
  How much time we'll be together
  Methods for meeting our objectives
  Information about our organization and about us
Gaining Information:
  Questions and other methods
Ending:
  What will happen with information after interview
  Your responsibilities after interview and his/hers
  Gaining commitment for what the person will do next

Let's go through the agenda item by item.

Here's the key part of the order of this agenda, what you'll always do:

- Start with a First Communication to get the person's attention to focus on the interview.
- End by gaining commitment for what the person will do next.

The *beginning* and the *ending* of the interview are most important because, as we'll learn in Chapter 6, whatever we say and do first and last has the most impact, since people retain it longer. Plan to get their attention as soon as they arrive and gain their commitment just before they leave—two things that are crucial to achieving the objectives of the interview.

The *First Communication* is your first words or actions. This is how you draw the person's attention from other matters so he or she focuses on the interview.

We've already planned our *objectives* and *how much time we'll be together.* We'll plan the other elements of the beginning and the complete ending, as well as the actual questions and methods for gaining the specific information in Chapter 6.

The Methods

The heart of the interview is *gaining information*, through questions and other methods.

We have many options in Chapter 3 for creating the variety of behavioral questions we need to keep the conversational flow. However, few interview objectives will be achieved solely through questions.

Some of the things you need to learn you can get more accurately by seeing than by hearing. (This is especially true for Expressives and Amiables, who find it easier to understand when they see things, as opposed to hearing them only.) Consider your information-gaining abilities and the person's information-giving abilities, then choose the best mix to reach your information and feeling objectives.

If you're not used to using methods other than questions to gain information, you're likely to think other methods always take more time. In fact, methods that allow you to *see* the information you need as well as *hear* it actually take less time. (A picture is worth a thousand words.) And even if other methods might take more time than questions, never trade accuracy for speed (unless the information you're gaining is about an imminent safety risk).

How do you choose your methods?

First, based on your objectives.

Choose for Accuracy and Efficiency

If you've found that using methods other than questions has taken longer, it may be that you needed to spend the time planning so you could implement them more efficiently. Or it may be that you needed to choose another method that would gain you accurate information in less time. If you're adept at several methods, it's easier to choose the one that'll give you accuracy and be most efficient!

Big List of Interviewing Methods

Before the Interview:

- Behavioral questions: asked verbally, answered in writing
- Behavioral questions: asked in writing, answered verbally
- Behavioral questions: asked in writing, answered in writing
- Writing sample
- Read information about organization, job, service, product or watch video, go to Web site, use CD, listen to audio
- Have references call
- Perform a task, use a product/service (see "Legal Issues," Chapter 5)
- Paper-and-pencil tests of aptitude, interests, needs

During the Interview:

- Behavioral questions: asked verbally, answered verbally
- Questions or other methods with several people beginning interview together
- Perform a task, use a product/service (see "Legal Issues," Chapter 5)
- Participate in a simulation of the task, product, service
- Watch a video or in-person simulation of the task, product, service
- Watch a task or the use of a product or a service being performed and tell the steps and/or give ideas for improvement
- Participate in a role-play and comment on specific things afterward
- Read/Hear a case study/story and tell steps, give ideas, comment on specific things afterward
- Take a tour of location
- Meet executives
- Meet other employees or customers
- Do things (assignments) after the interview

After the Interview:

- Field trip to another location to see a specific thing and call you with their ideas, questions

Any of these activities can be managed by a group of interviewers and/or by individual interviewers. Be sure to include these people in the planning process and help them learn to conduct a behavioral interview. (Use the forms and checklists in this book to help them.) Group interviewing is an excellent way for people you're interviewing from outside the organization—job candidates, prospective volunteers, customers, vendors—to learn about your organization. In addition, employees who would be working with those people can get to know them and provide input into the decision. It's a great start to building relationships.

Second, based on the person's best way to provide information.

Third (and only after you've done *everything* possible for the first two), based on available resources—time, people, equipment, supplies.

> **If the Customer Is Always Right ....**
> A well-known commercial airline flies in frequent fliers to interview candidates for employment. Since their company is built on customer relationships, the managers want to hire employees who match their customers' personalities.

Remember: it's easier for the person to give information if it's related to something he or she has done (the premise behind behavioral interviewing). So having a person do something is not only more accurate in many cases than just getting answers to questions, but also will be easier for the person (well, at least unless he or she is trying to keep information from you!).

Manager's Checklist for Chapter 4

❏ The proper planning and preparing saves time during the interview, shows the person you're interviewing that you consider the interview important, allows the person to prepare and thus feel more confident and comfortable, helps you reduce mistakes, and enables you to get the information you need, especially in situations where it may be difficult to get accurate information.

❏ Set information and feeling objectives. They should be in writing and SMART—meeting the criteria of specific, measurable, attained, realistic, and time.

❏ Determine and set the environment for the interview, using the checklists.

How Should I Prepare for the Interview?

In Chapter 4 you set your objectives, determined the environment, and planned your agenda and your methods (possibly including some you'll use before the interview). Now, it's time to develop that agenda outline into the Interview Planning and Conducting Tool that you'll use to prepare for the interview.

Gathering Information Before the Interview

Behavioral interviewing is a systematic process that's based on examples of past behavior. This means that much of what you need to know in order to achieve your information objectives you can get before you interview the person. Gathering information before the interview will not only save time for you and the person you're interviewing, but it's crucial to preparing.

What should you be looking for?

1. Information about communication style, past experiences, attitudes, beliefs, and values, so you can decide on what combination of methods to use for gaining information,

the most effective First Communication, and how you should ask questions.

2. Specific information that meets your information objectives (facts about past behavior related to the reason you're interviewing), so you can know how to set up the methods and what questions to ask to get the rest of the information you need.

Because you'll actually be making decisions based on the information you gather before the interview, you'll need to weigh it as carefully as the information you gain in the interview. (See Chapter 10.) First, write your objectives in your Interview Planning and Conducting Tool, so you know what information you're looking for. Then, gather the information and write what you learned in the "Information Gathered Before the Interview" section of the tool.

Information Gathered Before the Interview	
Communication Style Clues	**Information Gained That Meets the Information Objectives**
Past Experience, Attitudes, Beliefs, Values Related to the Reason for the Interview	

As you're gathering information, always:

- Distinguish fact from opinion.
- Verify the accuracy of the information you use.
- Retain the sources of your information.

What do you do with the source documents after using the information from them? You may use them in the interview to show the person—e.g., reports they wrote, forms they signed, booklets on what you're discussing, their résumé, and so on. Or they may simply help you prepare—e.g., letters from others giving you information.

You're always looking for information that meets your information objectives, but your sources will differ depending on the people you're interviewing and the reason for the interview (see chart for more on pages 94-95).

What to Communicate in Advance to Prepare the Person

When you provide some way for the person you're going to interview to know what to expect and to prepare for it, you create comfort for the person and you'll gain the information faster.

The only interviews that happen without any time to send or tell the person something ahead of time to prepare him or her are on-the-spot coaching with a direct employee or a peer or on-the-spot problem solving with customers. Even in most of these cases, you can still take a step back and have

Why Take Chances?

⚠️ CAUTION!

Write only information that relates to the objectives for this interview. That's the basic rule. Any other information you get is information you don't need to know to make the decisions—and exposes you unnecessarily to risks of legal action. (For more, see "Legal Issues" later in this chapter.)

the person look at something, read something, and/or hear something before you start the coaching or problem solving.

People/Reason for Interview	Where You'll Find Information
Candidates for Employment or Volunteer Work position/organization fit	Cover letter, résumé, application, written answers to questions, work samples, notes of contacts with candidate made before interview (calls, e-mails, formal phone pre-screen), paper-and-pencil or computer-based skill/knowledge testing, reference letters, notes/documents from reference checks
	Tell candidate to have references call you with specific information about his/her skills/knowledge that relate to the job description. Contact others who know his/her skills/abilities specific to job description, check accuracy of information given on résumé, application, and other sources cited above with organizations. (Contacts depend on what you're checking—e.g., schools attended, certifying bodies driver's license bureau.) Only, only, only if you need to know such information to determine if the person is able to do the job (see "Legal Issues" later in this chapter). Doing this as part of information gathering gives you valuable info for preparation and that you don't have to get in the interview.
Your Direct Employees performance appraisal, coaching, career development and planning	Employee file (memos, coaching notes, performance appraisals, hiring info, training info, career development plans), written performance appraisal or development plan (if that's the reason for the interview), documents with specifics about the event (if it's coaching), documents with info about options (procedure manual, training listing, etc.).
	If coaching, talk with anyone involved to confirm facts and details. Crucial to get their permission to reveal source of info. (When you say, "On Friday afternoon, Sam saw you doing ...," it creates an immediate, factual picture of the event and reduces defensiveness, as opposed to "I heard that....") Speak to HR staff (for advice, options, and, if coaching, how this type of incident has been handled in past), colleagues, and anyone with direct knowledge of the issue.
Peers strategic planning, problem solving	Past strategic plans, reports, mission, vision, values of organization, plans of other organizations/departments, articles/books about the issues.
	Talk with anyone involved to confirm facts and details. Contact colleagues and anyone with knowledge of the issue to get ideas for how they handled it.

Whatever time the person has to prepare for the interview, it's important for him or her to know in advance what's going to happen during the interview. In addition, in those on-the-spot

People/Reason for Interview	Where You'll Find Information
Current and Potential Customers focus groups, problem solving, discovering needs	Customer Web site, industry directories and other info on organization, customer file (letters, notes, contracts), instruction manuals for products/services, notes from contacts with person before interview (calls, e-mail, trouble reports).
	Speak to colleagues and anyone with knowledge of the person, the organization, the issue to confirm facts and details.
Vendors, Consultants, Colleagues ability to provide services to our organization, benchmarking	Cover letter, marketing materials, Web site, industry directories, Chamber of Commerce directory, applications, proposals, sample contracts, instruction booklets on using their products/services, reference letters, notes of contacts with person made before interview (calls, e-mails, formal phone pre-screen), reference letters, notes/documents from reference checks.
	Tell vendor/consultant to have others who've used their services/products call you with specific information about the work they did, how they completed it, what their outcomes have been. Contact others who know their abilities specific to what you're planning to buy. Check accuracy of information they've given on marketing documents, in contracts, and through phone contacts with organizations like the BBB.

situations, the few minutes the two of you take to stop and pre-pare will also serve as a space in which to calm down if either or both of you are angry. (More on this in Chapter 8.) Since you present it as "take a minute to look this over and prepare," you won't be adding to his or her anger by making a point of it. In any interview situation, preparation creates comfort for the person you're interviewing and you'll gain the information faster.

Things to Send or Tell People Ahead of Time

Below is a list of possibilities. Some you'll always do; others you'll choose to do based on the person, the reason for the interview, and the time between setting up the interview and conducting it.

- The interview agenda (do verbally, if it's impossible to get to them in writing in advance, and then ask them to write down what you're saying)

- Questions for them to answer in writing or verbally
- List of things for them to bring (work samples, past performance appraisal, filled-out appraisal form, work plan, sales receipts, specifications for product, etc.)
- Paper-and-pencil tests and written information, video, audio on product, service, job, organization (if not enough time to do at the interview, have alternative ways interviewee can get these items)
- Note or letter welcoming them

Keep your feeling and information objectives in mind when choosing what to communicate to the person and review them before you do, to be sure the person will receive it as you intend it. You're doing this to prepare the person so he or she will be comfortable. If you do something that causes confusion or irritation, you won't be meeting either of your objectives!

How much in advance of the interview should you send or tell the person? That depends on the following factors:

1. Who the person is (his or her schedule)
2. Why you're doing the interview (what does the person need to do? skim an agenda? read documents? take tests? write answers to questions? prepare an action plan? research a problem?)
3. How much time you have before the interview

Also, you need to think about keeping the amount of time required for preparation appropriate to your objectives.

Creating and Using the Interview Tools

We've been creating the interview tools throughout the planning process. In Chapter 2, you have the Communication Styles Expectations Tool and the Communication Styles Strategy Sheet to help you recognize and know how to modify to the person's style. In Chapter 3, you have the STAR Behavioral Interview Questions Worksheet to help you plan questions that allow you get information about Situations/Tasks, Actions, and Results from a past behavior. In this chapter, you have a variety of tools—for setting your objectives, preparing the environment, determining your agenda and methods, and gathering information before the interview.

The best interview tools are designed to *guide* you in planning and conducting the interview (especially for those situations when the interview is on the spot and there's no time for formal planning). The tools also need to *flow together easily* so they help you conduct the interview without juggling a bunch of papers. Finally, the tools need to allow *enough space* so you can write what you see and hear while still allowing you to pay attention, ask the questions in the way you've planned, transition to the next question or method, and avoid repeating questions for information you already have. Tall order?

The Interview Planning and Conducting Tool (pages 98-99) includes or references all the things you'll need to plan and conduct an interview that achieves your objectives in the most efficient, accurate manner.

The tool is worded generically enough that you can use it as the base for all your interviews, whether you're interviewing candidates for employment, coaching your employees or doing performance appraisals, strategic planning with peers, selling or solving problems with customers, or assessing vendors.

Busy people frequently ask, "How much time should I use for writing the plan and planning? (Oh, please don't tell me 'an hour'—I don't have it!)" My answer (you're not going to like this!) is that it depends on who you're interviewing and the reason for the interview. We've all heard we can save one minute for every two minutes we spend in planning, so a good rule of thumb is to spend twice as much time writing your plan and planning as you'll spend in the interview.

If you have the time, set a timer and work to beat the clock. This will help you avoid spending time beyond what's necessary. If you don't have the time, remember that any amount of planning is better than what you've been doing and that your interview tools make planning faster. They'll also guide you in conducting the interview if you plan only a little.

Interview Planning and Conducting Tool		
Our objectives Information: Feeling:		
What's in it for me:		

Beginning	**Words**
First communication:	Looking for:
Our information objectives:	
Their objectives:	
How much time we'll spend together:	Not looking for:
Methods for meeting objectives:	
Information about our organization and about us:	

Gaining Information			

Remember to transition from one question to the next to keep the interview from feeling choppy—ask a question or make a comment.

Information to Gain	STAR	Question (actions) or Other Method	What You Saw and Heard
	❑ Situation/ Tasks ❑ Actions ❑ Results		

Information to Gain	STAR	Question (actions) or Other Method	What You Saw and Heard
	❑ Situation/ Tasks ❑ Actions ❑ Results		

Information to Gain	STAR	Question (actions) or Other Method	What You Saw and Heard
	❑ Situation/ Tasks ❑ Actions ❑ Results		

Gaining Information			
Remember to transition from one question to the next to keep the interview from feeling choppy—ask a question or make a comment.			
Information to Gain	**STAR**	**Questions (actions) or Other Method**	**What You Saw and Heard**
	☐ Situation/ Tasks ☐ Actions ☐ Results		
Information to Gain	**STAR**	**Questions (actions) or Other Method**	**What You Saw and Heard**
	☐ Situation/ Tasks ☐ Actions ☐ Results		
Information to Gain	**STAR**	**Questions (actions) or Other Method**	**What You Saw and Heard**
	☐ Situation/ Tasks ☐ Actions ☐ Results		

Ending

Letting them know what will happen with this information after the interview.

Making sure they know what your responsibilities are after the interview as well as theirs.

Getting commitment from them for what they'll do next.

Person(s) Interviewed_____ **Date/Time**_____
Interviewer_____

We've just created a plan that will help us conduct a specific interview with a specific person. For some of the interviews we plan, such as for solving a particular problem, we'll never use any part of the plan again. For other interviews, particularly employment or sales (one on one or focus groups), we'll use the plan several times. You can customize the Interview Planning and Control Tool for each person/group you'll be inter-

What Do You Need?

You easily see how the Interview Planning and Conducting Tool applies to the different kinds of interviews, at least until the "Information to Gain" section. Then, this is what you need to get, depending on your situation:

- employment/volunteer/vendor interviews: "Information to Gain" is targeted behaviors
- coaching, performance appraisal, and career development planning: "Information to Gain" is targeted behaviors and how the person learns best
- strategic planning: "Information to Gain" is goals, methods to achieve and measure
- problem solving: "Information to Gain" is description of the real problem, possible solutions, solution action plan
- sales: "Information to Gain" is objectives, current situation, obstacles to objective, who needs services/products, budget, timelines

viewing. Information regarding communication style and past experiences may cause you to change the agenda order or the actions you'll use while asking a question or even delete or add a question, but you'll have a base from which to start. This will save you a lot of time. Also, for employment interviews, it will help you maintain equality in interviewing several people for the same position. (We'll discuss this point in the next section.)

Finally, your planning for any interview should include thinking of all the things that you might not expect and the way you'd react if a person acts in a way that's different from what you expect:

Time-Saving Planning Tips

- Set a timer for twice as much time as you expect to allow for the interview.
- First, write the interview plan as if it were a draft—as quickly as possible, whatever comes to you, without stopping to revise.
- Write the parts of the plan you're most comfortable with first.
- Write in pencil so you can make revisions.
- After you've filled out all parts of the interview planning tools, go back and revise the wording, modify the order, add or subtract things, and so on.

Key to Planning with the Interview Planning and Conducting Tool	
Interview Part	**How**
Our Objectives	see Chapter 4, pp. 69-78
What's in it for me	see Chapter 6, pp. 122-124
Information Gathered Before the Interview	see this chapter, pp. 91-93
Environment Checklist	see Chapter 4, pp. 78-86
Agenda	see Chapter 4, pp. 86-90
Beginning	see Chapter 6, pp. 112-127
Words	see Chapter 7, pp. 137-142
Information to Gain	see this chapter, pp. 96-100 and Chapter 7
STAR	use this to check that you've developed questions/ methods covering all three areas
Question (actions) or Other Method	for questions, see Chapter 3, pp. 45-60; for other methods, see this Chapter 4, pp. 88-90
What You Saw and Heard	see Chapter 7
Ending	see Chapter 6, pp. 127-130

- What could go wrong?
- What can I do to prevent it from happening?
- If it happens anyway, what can I do to fix it?

Legal Issues

We tend to think about legal issues in interviewing only in rela-
tion to hiring, but the best-known laws—anti-discrimination laws
based on protected classes of people—cover all aspects of the
employer-employee relationship. So in addition to candidates
for employment, anti-discrimination laws cover your direct
employees in performance appraisals and career development
interviews and your peers in strategic planning.

Anti-discrimination laws are only the beginning. There are
laws that govern what you need to do in order to hire non-U.S.

citizens. There are laws detailing what records you need to keep on potential, current, and former employees and for how long. Sexual harassment laws cover candidates for employment and volunteer work, your direct employees, your peers, and your boss. Some interviews with direct employees are for the purpose of terminating the employees; there are laws that govern how long you need to offer former employees access to health insurance. In performance appraisals of direct employees, you may be making decisions about compensation; how much to pay them and for what are covered by yet another law. You're interviewing in your offices a focus group of customers to find out their preferences for a certain product; now we're talking building codes, smoking laws, and physical liability. If you're interviewing vendors to decide among them and your company receives federal funds over a certain dollar amount, you're bound by regulations about what you require of vendors.

All of these laws and regulations come with paperwork to prove to various agencies that you didn't break the law. Shall I go on? This is why everyone thinks the whole area of legal issues of interviewing is such a nightmare!

Instead of throwing up my hands and moaning about the nightmare, I find it useful to continually remind myself of the reasons for these laws and regulations. They exist to help us humans (full of feelings, prejudices, and bad judgment and subject to bad days and poor planning) do things that will give us employees who can meet our customer needs, customers who are satisfied, and happy vendors who can serve us.

Let's take an example—interviewing candidates for a position as a word processor.

Interviewer: position's supervisor

Interview tools: a sheet of paper

Planning and preparation: was available for interview on time with said sheet of paper

Interview notes (on that sheet of paper): Chris Smith came to office on May 1 and took the word processing test—got 87

points. A current employee, Mary Jo, referred Chris, saying Chris was intelligent, resourceful, and ambitious. The candidate called before the interview and was told about the requirements of the position. Chris had only fairly good personal appearance and a good personality. Chris appeared to be intelligent, resourceful, and ambitious but appeared conceited. Doubt Chris would take discipline well. No hire.

What's wrong with this picture? Let's forget the obvious fact that this interviewer didn't use this book as a resource—little planning and preparation, an interview tool that's minimal. We can't comment on the objectives, the usefulness of the questions, or even the other methods, because there's nothing written down so we have no idea. (We know a test was used, but there are no specifics about what the test measured.) There's no way that candidates for the position could accurately be compared, because the process lacks structure. The outcomes (and we can only guess at what the interviewer expected) are written as the interviewer's opinions rather than as the candidate's behaviors or words.

> **Key Term**
>
> **EEOC—Equal Employment Opportunity Commission** The main U.S. government agency responsible for checking out employment discrimination claims relating to federal laws.
>
> There are also state and local government agencies that respond to claims of discrimination relating to state and local laws.

What's really wrong here? This interviewer made a decision based on a gut feeling, which regularly causes poor decisions—in this case, the wrong candidate hired or a great candidate missed. You're probably thinking, "Whoa, this is a lawsuit or an complaint waiting to happen!"

Of course, we're concerned about the legal issues because:

1. We're law-abiding citizens and don't want to break the law.
2. If we get caught, it costs time and money and bad publicity.
3. Even if we don't break the law, if someone files a claim it'll cost time and money and bad publicity to prove we didn't.

> ### Hierarchy of Laws
> All state laws in the U.S., if stricter than federal laws that relate to the same issue, take precedence over federal laws.
>
> All local laws in the U.S., if stricter than state laws, take precedence over state laws.
>
> Here's an example. A U.S. law prohibiting discrimination in employment doesn't include discrimination based on whether or not a person smokes cigarettes. However, your state has a law prohibiting discrimination in employment that includes all the protected classes of people listed in the federal law—plus people who smoke. You are bound by the state law.

Let's first be concerned about making bad decisions for our organizations. If we take this approach, it's quite unlikely that we'll break any laws. You decide: is it a good decision to pass up an employee who can do the job well because of our own feelings about his or her cultural background? Is it a good decision to maintain safety and health risks in our offices and buildings? Is it a good decision to work with vendors who discriminate against their employees? Of course not.

So, besides a lot of time-consuming paperwork, what is it about the laws we don't like? Nothing. Do I wish there were fewer laws and therefore less paperwork? You bet! But since we have the laws, we can use them as procedures for making great business decisions.

> ### Equal Opportunity
> It is illegal to discriminate against a person based on various criteria (e.g., sexual orientation, race, color, national origin, religion, age, sex). The laws apply to any aspect of employment; discrimination may take the form of not hiring a candidate or not promoting an employee or compensating one employee less than another or giving an employee a more severe punishment.

The vast majority of legal issues—code for "procedures for making great business decisions"—relating to interviewing have to do with the decisions we make with the information we gain in the interviewing process. Here's the basic rule: *get only the informa-*

> ### It's Not What You Seek ...
> The key concepts for avoiding legal issues are the verbs **Smart**
> "get," gain," and "have/had." People say that you must avoid **Managing**
> illegal questions in an interview with a candidate for employment.
> However, there are no laws in the U.S.—none—that make it illegal to
> ask any questions. It's not asking the question, it's having the informa-
> tion!
> Of course you need to ask only "need to know" questions and use
> methods that will get you "need to know" information. But if you get
> the information because the person gives it to you, even if you didn't
> ask, you have it.

tion you need to meet your information objectives. Any other information you get is information you don't need to know to make the decisions (who to hire, what to do about a perform-ance problem, what action steps to take to solve a problem, what services a customer needs, what vendor to contract with).

If the person you interview feels the information you have about him or her and/or about the organization that he or she represents has caused you to make an unfavorable decision—this never happens with *favorable* decisions—the person or the organization may go out looking for a law that covers the issue. If you get only information that meets your objective (and your information objective is set very specifically based on tasks in a job description or requirements for a vendor), the person or the organization can look for a law and maybe even begin the process of using that law to get you to change your decision, but you will have evidence that you had only information you needed to make a decision based on a very specific set of objectives.

Here are a few recommendations for getting only the informa-tion you need to and using it to make good business decisions:

1. Keep chitchat to safe topics, like the weather or traffic. Avoid asking, for example, what the person did last week-end. That question might lead him or her to mention church activities, which would provide information you don't want, because religion is a protected basis. You can-

not know the person's religion—unless he or she is applying for a job for which being of a certain religion would be a bona fide occupational qualification.

2. Write information objectives that are specific to what you must know to make a decision (see pp. 70-76).

3. Write questions that get you only the information you need to know (see Chapter 3) and use them for all the interviews for the same objectives.

4. Use other interviewing methods that get you only the information you need to know (see Chapter 1, pp. 9-11 and from Chapter 4, pp. 88-90) and use them for all the interviews for the same objectives.

Having a candidate for employment actually perform a task is an excellent method for determining if he or she can do it. However, most state department of labor laws make it clear that you need to pay a candidate for doing any work that would have been done by a paid employee. In most organizations, the only reasonable way to pay someone is to put the person on the payroll. But doing so involves plenty more laws (like unemployment and worker's comp) if the new employee does the task and then it's determined that he or she isn't able to do the job.

To avoid this situation, set up real work that will never benefit the company, because it's not done for a customer. For example, a hotel manager who wants to determine how well and quickly a candidate can clean a guest room could keep one room in the hotel that no guests ever use. The manager or an employee would mess up the room as if an average guest had stayed there. The candidate would clean it. Then it would be messed up the same way for the next candidate.

5. If the person starts to tell you something you don't need to know and it relates to any protected classes, say, "Joe, I want to keep us on track with the information relating to ..." *and then restate the question or ask the next.*

6. Use your interview tools to be sure you've planned only

Keep up with the Law

New laws, changes to laws, new case law, guidelines that interpret laws, and new regulations come into being every day and are different from locality to locality. What can you do?

Learn the major laws relating to your area of interviewing. Here's a great place to start: www.uslaw.com.

Keep up with new information and changes by subscribing to legal publications in your area of interviewing—employment, customer sales, direct employee. Start with Rominger Legal, at www.romingerlegal.com.

Have access to an attorney in your area of interviewing who can answer your questions. Use the expert information services of the trade association in your industry. Learn about trade associations from the American Society of Association Executives, www.asaenet.org.

Smart Managing

"need to know" questions/methods, to get back on track if the person starts to tell you things you don't need to know, and to write the information (words or behaviors) you got relating to the specific objectives.

Note: all six recommendations are what we've advised throughout the book to get the most accurate information quickly and comfortably for everyone involved.

Remember: the need to gain only information you need to know applies to the entire process, from gathering information before the interview (see pp. 91-93) through following up after the interview (see Chapter 10).

Another area of legal issues in interviewing has to do with all the supporting documents and interview tools we use. There are time periods for which you must keep the different kinds of documents—paper and electronic. These time periods relate to the length of time during which a person or an organization has the right to make a claim that you've broken a law.

If you don't keep records long enough or in the right location or you get and use information you don't need to know or allow people to come into your unsafe spaces, it's likely to be because you just didn't know. In the legal system, this is rarely a defense that works, so let's instead be on the offense.

Putting It All Together

So let's summarize the steps for planning and preparing for your interview. In going through this list, remember, planning is doing all the things upstream that makes everything downstream go well.

- Set objectives.
- Gather information ahead.
- Set environment and time based on objectives and who you're interviewing.
- Set agenda and methods.
- Create beginning, questions/methods, and ending.
- Communicate information in advance so the person is prepared.

You're ready!

Manager's Checklist for Chapter 5

❏ Gather information before the interview, to save time and to prepare more effectively.

❏ Communicate in advance to the person whatever he or she needs in order to know what to expect and how to prepare for the interview, so you'll gain the information you seek faster and more easily.

❏ Know about the laws and regulations that apply to interviews. They help us do things that will give us employees who can meet our customer needs, customers who are satisfied, and happy vendors who can serve us.

How Should I Begin and End the Interview?

A bad beginning makes a bad ending.
　　　　　—Euripides

The beginning is the most important part of the work.
　　　　　—Plato

He who has begun has half done.
　　　　　—Horace

The beginning of the interview is the most important part. It's where you'll make the process either long and uncomfortable or efficient and pleasant. In the first few seconds, people make decisions about you, your organization, and their ability to work with you. If you create comfort and gain commitment to participate in the first few seconds, you'll be able to move forward easily with your plan. You do this by knowing the person you're interviewing and that person's communication style and therefore how you'll begin in a way that makes him or her comfortable.

If you were able to get specific information about the person in the planning process (Chapter 4), you're ready to go. If you have only general information, you'll use your ability to recognize communication styles and modify on your feet. Your planning process helps you because you've created the atmosphere that will make the person feel comfortable immediately and you've planned the objectives so it'll be easy for the person to know the purpose of this interview. Knowing about the person, creating the atmosphere, and beginning with the objectives will allow you to achieve those objectives comfortably and efficiently.

The ending is as crucial to achieving the objectives as the beginning: people remember the first and the last things we say and/or do (*primacy-recency effect*). We'll therefore work in this chapter on the beginning and the ending at the same time, since they have the greatest impact on our ability to achieve the objectives of the interview. They also tend to be the parts of any interview that are planned least (before this book, of course!) and thus you're likely to benefit greatly from this chapter.

The planning process and the resulting interview tools you created in Chapters 4 and 5 get you ready to begin. Using the interview tools, you planned the major points to cover at the *beginning*:

- information about your organization and about you

Primacy-recency effect The natural tendency of people to remember best what comes first and what comes last.

Numerous studies in the 1920s (F.H. Lund, Arthur Jersild, F.H. Knower) found that the information presented first will have a greater effect than the information presented subsequently (primacy). Numerous studies in the 1950s (H. Cromwell, Carl I. Hovland, and Wallace Mandell) found just the opposite: the information presented most recently has a greater effect than information presented before it (recency).

The debates go on and on, with researchers finding evidence for primacy and for recency. Many practitioners choose the practical perspective, that in any situation they should plan to say and do the most important things first and last.

- your objectives
- the other person's objectives
- how much time the two of you will be together
- the method for meeting your objectives

Now you have to say these things in the order that makes it easiest for the person you're interviewing to understand in this situation and to create the impact you desire (to achieve your objectives). If you had a lot of specific information about the person during the planning process, this order would be already set before the beginning of the interview. If not, you'll be setting a general order in the planning process and modifying as necessary during the beginning of the interview.

You also planned the things you need to cover in the *ending*:

- letting the other person know what will happen with the information after the interview
- making sure the person knows his or her responsibilities and your responsibilities
- gaining commitment from the person for what he or she will do next

Now, you've got a wonderful plan, so the interview should be effective, efficient, and easy, right? Well, not quite.

Although the plan and the tools you've created are crucial, you need to work to implement the plan and use the tools appropriately. In implementing the plan, you'll use your abilities to recognize and modify to the person's communication style (Chapter 2) and any differences in experiences, attitudes, beliefs, and values (Chapter 2) and your knowledge of how to ask the questions (Chapter 3) you planned in your interview tools. What you planned and what actually happens will be more similar when you conduct the planned beginning and ending portions of the interview with intentional actions (facial expressions, body movements, tone of voice, emphasis on certain words, pauses, and the words you choose) that are always, always, always focused on the person you're interviewing and the objectives to be achieved.

The Beginning: Gaining Attention and Creating Comfort

You've planned the environment so there are few distractions. You've created a comfortable atmosphere. You've set the time so it's long enough to gain the information at a fast pace so no one gets bored. You've given the person information ahead of time so he or she is prepared for what you'll be doing together. You're planning to modify to the person's communication style. You're going to use behaviorally based questions. You've done everything in the first five chapters to make it easy and enjoyable for the person you're interviewing so it'll be easy for him or her to give you the information you need. So what else is there to gaining attention and creating comfort?

Unexpected Beginnings

Be prepared to help calm the person or to stay calm yourself if something unexpected happens before the interview. It could be that the person arrives late, that you arrive late, that he or she is excessively nervous, that you're nervous, that he or she didn't get or didn't understand the information you provided in advance, that you didn't prepare like you know you should. It could even be that the other person has a very different picture about how giving and gaining information should happen.

Here are things to do in some of the most common unex-

Amazing but True

A candidate for employment got off to a shaky start before the interview began. The candidate was shown to the manager's workspace while the manager was down the hall getting copies of materials for the interview. When the manager returned to her office, she found the candidate looking through papers on her desk! She was amazed!

In as calm a voice as she could muster, the manager asked the candidate what he was doing. The candidate very matter-of-factly said he was trying to learn as much as he could about the manager and the organization before the interview.

pected pre-interview situations that will help you and the person you're interviewing get calm and be able to begin the interview. Remember to apply what you know about his or her communication style to these general ideas.

The person arrives late. He or she will be flustered, not a good state for giving accurate information concisely. If the person wants to explain the whole story to you (more likely with Amiables and Expressives, but possible with Analyticals and Drivers since the pressure might put them in their backup styles), let him or her talk for about 30 seconds (enough time to get it out of their systems and to feel that you're interested but not so long as to lose even more time or venture into areas of information you don't need to know). Then, say something like "This can happen to anyone" or, if it's true, that it's happened to you and immediately move into "I'm so looking forward to hearing about ...." (the topic objective). State how much time you'll be together. (If less than originally planned, simply say, "We now have ... minutes." Avoid using the words "We only have ...."). Then, go forward with the rest of your plan.

If this is a group interview, such as a focus group of customers or a planning meeting of colleagues, start on time. When somebody arrives late, simply welcome the person into the group and point out any written information that will help him or her catch up. Avoid catching somebody up in front of the group, as this will penalize the people who were on time. Of course, the latecomer may not be able to give as much information as if he or she had arrived on time or you'd got him or her up to speed, but you're more likely to get information from the group if you move forward.

If this is an interview with a candidate for employment or volunteer work or a vendor or consultant, the person's lateness may affect your assessment of him or her. Avoid making the decision now. Remember: the objectives for this interview are to gain a particular piece of information and create a certain feeling, not to make a decision to hire or not. Stick to the objectives and you'll achieve them!

You arrive late. The first words out of your mouth will always be "I apologize for keeping you waiting," immediately followed by how much you're looking forward to hearing about ... . (the topic objective) and telling the person how much time you'll be together (minus the word "only"). If you've chosen to spend the same amount of time as originally planned, it's important to ask the person if this fits his or her schedule. If not, you'll need to modify the method you planned for getting information now or just start and then modify at the end, if necessary. Either way, tell how the interview will work just as if this was the way you planned it (as opposed to saying, "Well, now that I was late we'll have to ..."). Say "I'm sorry" only once at the beginning; saying it more will only prolong your discomfort. Moving right into your plan (potentially changed slightly if you have less time) will help you to calm down. (If the other person is irritated that you're late or concerned about the time, calm him or her down, too.) Your ability to get calm will create comfort in the person you're interviewing, thus allowing him or her to give information, which in turn further calms you down.

Make no mistake: behaving calmly doesn't mean going extra slowly or pausing a lot or with a look on your face like you're on vacation in a beautiful island paradise. This behavior makes irritated people more irritated. Being calm means your voice is steady (not high-pitched, cracking, or fast), which exhibits confidence that'll translate to the person who's been waiting for you.

The person is nervous. Most interviewers try to deal with this situation by adding "small talk" at the beginning. This may eventually calm the person down, if he or she is an Amiable or an Expressive, but it will take longer to get the information. On the other hand, if the person is a Driver or an Analytical, it'll irritate him or her. Instead, use your planned beginning and pause after the objectives to look for comprehension, then restate if you still see panic. (It should be pretty obvious.) Restating the objectives will help calm the person. (Repetition in itself is calming, like the use of a mantra in meditation or prayer.) If he or she was too nervous to take in the objectives the first time, restating allows another chance. Writing is also a calming activity (since it involves the left half of the brain—center of reason and logic—more than the right half—center of emotions and spatial relationships), so you can suggest that the person write the objectives or, if you're sharing the interview tools with him or her and the objectives are already written, circle them.

Keep going with your plan. Since you're asking questions that are behavioral, about past experiences, the person has only to recall, not create answers. Though the first few sentences may be rushed or choppy, he or she will at least feel able to answer your questions about past experiences. It's their story, not your answer. The person will become more confident. You can help him or her relax by taking notes, nodding, maintaining eye contact, leaning forward, and the other active listening behaviors that we'll discuss in Chapter 7.

> **Left Brain/Right Brain**
>
> **Smart Managing**
>
> In the late 1960s, Roger W. Sperry, a neurobiologist who won a Nobel Prize in 1981, advanced a theory of the structure and working of the brain that suggests that the two sides ("hemispheres") of the brain control different "modes" of thinking and for different people one or the other of these modes is more dominant. This theory has since been investigated, confirmed through experiments, and further developed.

You're nervous. Take a deep breath and speak in a slightly lower pitch and at a slightly slower pace than usual. When you're nervous, the pitch of your voice tends to get higher (hence the squeaky, sometimes cracking voice as you're out of your vocal range) and you speak more rapidly. You know that you sound nervous, so you become even more nervous. Consciously slowing down your pace and lowering your pitch can fake you out long enough to allow you to gain some confidence. As you hear your voice become more normal, you begin to feel the way you sound. Of course, as the other person responds to you based on the way you sound, it helps you feel like you're conveying confidence. Stand up straight, with your hands out of your pockets, and without crossing your arms. This posture conveys confidence, so the person reacts to you as though you were feeling confident. Soon you'll actually feel confident.

The person didn't get the information you gave ahead of time. If it was by voice mail, simply say, "I apologize that you didn't get a chance to hear the info I wanted you to have before you got here. What I said was ...." Then ask, "What questions do you have, as I want to be sure you're prepared before we begin?" You need to allow enough silence here for the person to think about what you said and formulate any questions. (This is hard to do, as silence seems like an eternity. You may want to excuse yourself for a minute to give the person time to think, saying, "I'll be back in a minute to answer any questions you have.")

If the information was something to read (e-mail, fax, mail), give the person a copy and again say, "Take a few minutes"—or whatever time you feel is needed—"and I'll be back to answer any questions you might have so you'll be prepared to begin."

In either case, answer any questions and then begin using your prepared plan.

What if you're interviewing a group of people and only one or a few didn't get the information in advance? If you gave the information by voice mail, use the same tactic as in the earlier example of when members of a group arrive late. If you gave the information in writing, use the tactic described above, but instead of leaving, give them a space in another room close by and a few minutes to prepare, telling them to come back when they've read the information. Then, begin with the rest of the group as planned. This will cause them to miss a few minutes, but they'll be better able to give information even after missing the first minutes than if they stay but aren't prepared.

The person didn't understand the information you gave in advance. You'll probably not know this until you've begun using your planned beginning and either hear or see something that tells you the person didn't understand the objectives or the time or his or her role in meeting the objectives. Once you discover this, get out the written information you provided, give the person another copy (if necessary), and say, "What I planned for you to know/understand is different from what you do, so let's look at what I sent you and see where we differ." Then say what you meant and ask for questions, just like above when the person didn't get the information. If you provided the information verbally, use the same tactic (minus giving a copy, of course). Once you both have the same understanding, begin again (since your beginning made no sense the first time).

You didn't prepare sufficiently. Get out blank interview tool forms and follow the general agenda for any interview. Write the questions you ask as you ask them, note the person's communication style and the modifications you need to make, and use the tools for recording, as usual. Is this optimal? Will you be able to be as concise and to create as much comfort as if you'd prepared sufficiently? No, but having the tools will give you a fighting chance. The tools (even blank as they are when you begin) are some of the preparation; they're just not specific to this particular interview.

The person has a very different picture of the interview process. People come to interviews—whether for jobs or for performance appraisals or for discussing doing business—with their own history of giving and gaining information. No matter how well you explain the objectives ahead of time, you may not create the understanding you planned if the person's picture of the process from past experience is wildly different than yours.

In Chapter 2 we discussed how communication styles affect the ways that people understand a process and the effects of experiences, attitudes, beliefs, and values. As we saw, we can benefit from recognizing and predicting, but even with the best preparation you must be prepared to think on your feet. (For example, there was nothing in my pre-interview data gathering that would have prepared me for the candidate who was shuffling the papers on my desk. Yes, that manager was me!)

The only advice I have for you here is to read a lot of horror stories about the kinds of people and situations in which you'll be interviewing (job applicants, direct employees with perform-ance and career development needs, strategic planning with peers, sales and customer service or vendors and colleagues). This will at least keep you from being so amazed that you can't function!

First, respond to the person's behavior. (In the example above, I asked the candidate what he was doing, he responded, and I said, "I appreciate you wanting to be prepared and I'd be glad to give you the information you need instead of you having to look for it on my desk.") Then, begin the interview. Again, stick to achieving the objectives and leave your decision-mak-ing process for later.

That's not easy, I realize, but unless the person poses a threat, you'll achieve both objectives—information and feeling—by moving forward as planned. I've done interviews for employ-ment, performance appraisals, and sales that would have turned out poorly for me and for the organization if I'd reacted to the unexpected before the interview and not followed through with my plans.

Note: All of the above you absolutely must say with the utmost sincerity in order to make the person feel comfortable enough to give you information. Make eye contact. Smile. Show a sympathetic facial expression while listening to his or her story. Stand up straight with arms at your side—or anywhere but crossed or with your hands in your pockets. Speak in an even tone of voice—not too fast paced (excited), not too slow/deliberate (angry, bored).

There are, of course, many other things that can happen before the interview and threaten to throw your plan off. How comfortably you interact with people before the unexpected occurs will give you insight into areas in which you're excellent and want to emphasize and areas in which you need to improve.

Of course you're prepared to talk with the people you inter-view, but do you really feel comfortable? Check "yes" or "no" for the following questions. As you do so, think about what others would say about you for each. Better yet, photocopy this exercise, complete it, and then ask someone else to complete it about you. This will give you a truer picture.

How Comfortable Are You Interacting with Others?		
Yes	**No**	
❏	❏	1. Do you smile when you meet and talk with people?
❏	❏	2. Are you really interested in people and what they do?
❏	❏	3. Do you greet people as soon as you see them?
❏	❏	4. Do you call by name most people whose names you know?
❏	❏	5. Do you offer to help others?
❏	❏	6. Do you feel patient with people?
❏	❏	7. Do you display a good sense of humor?
❏	❏	8. Do you give praise when someone's done something to warrant it?
❏	❏	9. Are you patient when people are talking, even long-winded people, and do you avoid finishing their sentences?
❏	❏	10. Do you look for the possible ways to handle a problem instead of feeling angry that it happened or like there's no way to solve it?
❏	❏	11. Do you think about others' feelings before saying or doing something?
❏	❏	12. Do you try to be positive rather than negative when expressing yourself?
❏	❏	13. Do you avoid criticizing people if possible?

Now, compare both sets of checks (yours and the person with whom you're doing this). Look at the questions for which there are two "yes" checks. Circle the one that's your "ultimate yes"—the behavior you really excel at. Now look at the questions for which you have two "no" checks. Circle the one you feel would make the biggest difference in your ability to interact comfortably when you improve it. These are the two areas to work on right away. Get better at your best points, to compensate for your weaker points. At the same time, of course, work on those weaker points. Interviewers who interact comfortably with others can smooth over the most unexpected things and get ready for a great beginning to the interview no matter what else is happening.

Determining First Communication

The person you're interviewing is now in the chair in your office or the people are assembled around a conference table or you're now in the person's office. And you've either passed the unexpected pre-interview issues described on the previous pages or everything has gone as expected. You're ready to begin.

The way you begin will be a bit different depending on who's in the interview and for what reason you're interviewing. You'll always cover the major points listed earlier in the chapter for what to do at the beginning but in a different order or in different combinations and with different emphasis. There are two exceptions to covering all the points: direct employees and peers. (See the matrixes below.)

Just before the interview, the person was involved in something else (working on other things, talking to other people, driving to your office). In order for the person to be able to participate from the very first moment, you need to gain his or her attention away from those other matters and focused on the interview. In show business and sales, it's called a *hook*. In training, it's called the *attention-getting opening*.

What will get the people's attention in the interviews you're conducting will be different based on two variables—the person's communication style and the reason for the interview.

If you know the person and thus his or her communication style, use the Communication Style First Communication Matrix (Figure 6-1) combined with the Reason for Interviewing First Communication Matrix (Figure 6-2) to determine what we need to start with to gain his or her attention.

If you are meeting the person for the first time and had no way to gain information before the interview on his or her most comfortable way of communicating, use only the Reason for Interviewing First Communication matrix to determine the first communication and the order for the rest of the beginning. Lucky you if you had an unexpected beginning, as it allows you to recognize the person's communication style, so you can use the style as part of your First Communication and thus improve your ability to gain his or her attention, away from the uncomfortable, unexpected event.

	Driver	Expressive	Amiable	Analytical
Face/Body	OK to have longer eye contact; resting face; few gestures	OK to have longer than usual eye contact; excited face, smiling when appropriate; wide, sweeping, fast gestures	Shorter than usual eye contact; smiling when appropriate; calm face; gestures are slow but many	Shorter than usual eye contact; resting face; few gestures
Voice	Fast paced; pause only for extreme emphasis; a bit louder than normal	Fast paced; no pauses; very positive, upbeat; a bit louder than normal	Slower than usual; pause for emphasis frequently; calm and caring; a bit softer than normal	Slower with careful enunciation; pause for emphasis frequently; calm and in control; normal volume
Words	Nouns and verbs; few and to the point; verb first **Start with:** The time and objectives as one sentence: e.g., "We'll be together for 30 minutes so you can give me information on how your experience and skills fit with the position."	Lots of adjectives and adverbs; to the point; positive **Start with:** The method and objectives as one sentence: e.g., "We'll be exchanging ideas about how your experience and skills fit with the position."	Lots of adjectives and adverbs; many words descriptive of people **Start with:** Brief information about yourself and the organization: e.g., "I'm ..., the manager of ... and at ... organization, we ...."	Factual, measurable, specific; many words **Start with:** The objectives and the method for achieving them: e.g., "I need to know about how your experiences and skills fit with the position, and we'll do this using a combination of ...."

Figure 6-1. Communication Style First Communication Matrix

Notice that the objectives are a part of the words of the First Communication in every situation for interviewing, but handled a bit differently in order to grab attention in that specific situation, depending on communication styles and/or the reason for the interview. Gain attention and create comfort by choosing your First Communication to match the communication style of the person, his or her position and relationship to you, and the reason for the interview.

We now have the order for the beginning and the words for

When Interviewing:	Start With	Order for Rest of Beginning
Candidates for Employment or Volunteer Work	Objectives (e.g., Today we'll be exploring your experiences and skills as they relate to the position)	Time Methods Their objectives Information about the organization and yourself
Your Direct Employees	Objectives (e.g., You and I will be identifying the specific skills and tasks at which you excel and the ones that aren't your forte and developing methods for enhancing both)	Time Methods Their objectives
Peers	Objectives (e.g., Do you want to decrease rework this quarter by 10%? We'll give each other ideas for how)	Time Methods Their objectives
Current and Potential Customers	Objectives (e.g., You'll be giving us information on how product X has performed for you)	Time Methods Brief information about the organization and yourself Their objectives
Vendors, Consultants, Colleagues in Other Organizations	Brief information about the organization and the objectives as a single sentence (e.g., ABC Company provides ... and in order to continue this cost-effectively we need information about your ... services)	Time Methods Brief information about the organization and yourself Their objectives

Figure 6-2. Reason for Interviewing First Communication Matrix

the various parts of the beginning are planned into our interviewing tools. Let's look at the issues related to delivering them.

Presenting Objectives

In Chapter 4, you set two types of objectives: an *information* objective (to gain a particular piece of information) and a *feeling* objective (to have the person you interview feel a certain way after the interview).

With candidates for employment and vendors, consultants, and colleagues in other organizations, you'll be stating only the

information objective. The feeling objective would sound manip-
ulative to these two groups: e.g., "I want you to feel like we're a
wonderful place to work and tell all your friends even if we
decide after that this isn't the right match for you."

For direct employees, peers, and current and potential customers, you would also state the second objective, because
doing so adds to your ability to achieve the objective: e.g., "We
want you to feel your issues have been heard."

The reason for actually stating objectives is so the other person knows where we're going and can help us get there, both
by doing things that meet the objectives and by calling us on
directions that the interview is taking that aren't meeting the
objectives. By stating the feeling objective to direct employees,
peers, and current and potential customers, you're giving them
permission to correct you if they're not feeling as you want
them to feel.

Stating the information objective also focuses all the people
involved on a similar picture of the outcome of the interview. It
allows you to know immediately whether you and the other person have the same picture.

If the other person thought he or she was there to do something else, you'll know it, because the person will immediately
tell you what he or she thought (so you won't need to ask) or
convey a feeling of surprise in his or her facial expression and/or
voice (so you will ask about his or her objectives for the interview right away, instead of following the order you'd planned).

What should you do if you hear an objective that doesn't
match?

Immediately affirm that objective—"I understand that your
picture of what we'd be doing today is…"—instead of saying,
"I'm sorry I misled you" or "That's not the objective." Then say,
"My picture is" and restate your objective. Then say, "Let's look
at where these overlap and choose which pieces of each we can
do in the 30 minutes we planned."

In the process of looking for overlaps, it's likely you'll find
the objectives are very similar but expressed in different words.

If they really are different, then the two of you need to decide if you're going to extend the time to achieve both or if you'll achieve parts of each now and then plan how to achieve the rest in another interview or with another method (i.e., by phone or in writing).

In order to meet both the information objective and the feeling objective, you'll need to be sure you've aligned your objectives before you move on with your plan. A person who feels that you don't consider his or her objectives important enough to address them will have a hard time giving you concise and accurate information—and the inability to meet the feeling objective is obvious.

Stating Time and Methods

After objectives, you mention how long the interview will take and the methods by which you'll be achieving the objectives.

Simply state the time, without any judgments. Never say "*only* 45 minutes," "a *whole* hour," "a *short* hour," "This could take as long as...," "I'll get you out of here in...," or "We won't need more than...."

Describe the methods you'll be using in terms of the person's communication style. No matter how many ways you'll be gaining information (asking questions, giving a tour, showing a video or other example, writing plans, etc.), follow these guidelines so the method is understandable and appealing to the person:

- Drivers—"You'll be giving me the information by first ...." (Tell the first method only.)
- Expressives—"We'll be using lots of different methods." (List all the methods.)
- Amiables—"We'll have lots of opportunities to share views with each other through ...." (List all the methods.)
- Analytical—"We'll be using a combination of methods to get the information we need." (List all the methods.)

For candidates for employment, peers, direct employees, and customers, now is the time to get the person to state his or her objectives (unless you had an alignment conversation and took care of that).

Since I've taken much of this chapter to cover the first several parts of the beginning of the interview, you might feel like it takes up most of the interview time! In fact, if you have no unexpected pre-interview issues and your objectives are aligned, the part of the beginning we've worked on so far looks like this:

> You and I will be identifying the specific skills and tasks at which you excel and the ones that aren't your forte and developing methods for enhancing both. We'll use the performance appraisal tool to identify and write how you perform each skill and task for the next hour. Tell me what you expect to leave this conversation with. (*The person will probably tell you in about three sentences.*)

If you have to align objectives or deal with lateness or nervousness, the above two to five minutes might become 10-15 minutes.

Telling About Your Organization and Yourself

The amount of time you spend telling the person about your organization and yourself is important. Too much and you bore the person and take valuable time that should be spent getting information from him or her. Too little time and the person doesn't have enough information and/or feel comfortable enough to give you the information you're seeking.

If you know whether you tend to give too little or to give too much and why you do so, you can overcome your tendency and stick to your plan.

If you tend to give *too little* information:

- You may be more interested in getting information than in telling things you know.
- You may be new to your organization and don't feel you have enough information.
- You may not be pleased with your job or some aspect of

your organization so you don't want to talk about it.

- You may have spent too much time in past interviews telling about your organization so you're trying to cut back.

If you tend to give *too much* information:

- You may not have done enough planning so you fill the time telling things instead of gaining information.
- You may be so excited about your job and organization you just can't stop talking about them.
- You may be Amiable, Analytical, or Expressive and so you need to give lots of information or you feel others need to have it.

Never assume that the person knows about you and about your organization. Of course, if it's one of your direct employees or a peer, you don't have to give your name or a history of the organization, but referencing a piece of information about you or the organization that relates to the reason for the interview will do what the beginning is intended to do—get the attention of the person and set the stage.

If the person might have been expecting someone else to conduct the interview (such as a performance appraisal or a problem-solving session), tell why it's you rather than someone perhaps more involved in the situation. This keeps potentially hot situations cool by anticipating and answering in advance the question on the person's mind: "Why isn't it _____ talking with me?" (See Chapter 8.)

Here are some points to include, depending on who you're interviewing and the reason for the interview:

- organization's values, mission, vision, plans
- major products and services
- customers
- number of employees
- locations
- major accomplishments
- brief history

Make It Easy and Effective

TRICKS OF THE TRADE

If you're having a difficult time determining what to say about the organization and yourself in the interview:

• Remember that shorter is better than longer.
• Ask yourself a question about the person's motivation: e.g., "Why would the person want to work here?" "Why would the person want to give this information?" "Why would the person want to change his or her behavior?"
• Send or tell the person some information in advance of the interview.
• Use the bulleted list above and write something for each point. Then shorten each and put first the things that relate to the reason for the interview—and then you may even decide to delete the rest!

• opportunities and benefits of working with you
• your role, your history

Keep the person or people you'll be interviewing in mind at all times. What do they need to know in order to feel comfortable, so it's easy to give information you need? What do they want to know?

Watch their reactions as you're telling them and condense if you're getting cues (see Chapter 7) that you're giving more information than they need to know or that they already know the information. If they want more, give them as much as you can while watching the time so you can keep to your agenda.

The Ending: Gaining Commitment

We place a great amount of importance on the beginning of the interview. If you don't gain the attention of the person and make him or her comfortable, it'll be impossible for you to achieve your objective, which leads to the end of the interview.

And then what happens? By the time you reach the end of the interview, you've been racing the clock, managing your questions, listening, taking notes, and managing all the tendencies you're trying to improve or overcome. Even if the interview has been fun, even if you've achieved all of your objectives, even if it's been going like clockwork, you have another interview or another task to do next and so you cut your ending short: "Bye, thanks for coming, I'll let you know what happens." That may happen even though you've planned an ending.

Sometimes we may let the clock, schedules, and/or our feelings cause us to skip the planned ending. And if you have to skimp on something, better the end than the beginning, where you set the scene, or the middle, where you gain the information. Right?

Without the well-planned and properly executed *beginning*, there is no ending. But without the well-planned and properly executed *ending*, you'll have a hard time achieving the feeling objective for this interview and both the feeling objective and the information objective in the future. Candidates and volunteers who have friends who might be just right for your organization might not recommend it. Your direct employees and peers might be less likely to give accurate information easily the next time. Your customers might be less likely to help you again or to buy from you. Though your vendors may keep coming back, they might do so with less enthusiasm when you call.

It's difficult to gain commitment if you skip the ending.

Explaining How the Information Will Be Used

When you let the person know how the information you gained from him or her will be used, it signals that you've achieved your objectives and the interview is coming to an end. A person who knows what's planned is more likely to be willing to give information in the future.

The explanation is also important for gaining commitment from the person for anything you need him or her to do next. A person who knows how the information will be used is more likely to feel like doing his or part as well. Again, you're meeting the feeling objective now and making it easier to achieve information objectives in the future.

Pause after explaining how the information will be used, in case the person has questions. Remember: the information he or she just gave you may be very personal (as with a job candidate) or confidential (as with a direct employee) or the outcome of your use of the information may be very important to the person (as in problem solving). It's really important that your face, body, and tone of voice communicate the message, "Ask me any questions and be sure you understand exactly what will happen," as opposed to a rushed look that says, "No time now!"

In Chapters 4 and 5 we planned what we'd do and how we'd say what we'll do with the information. Now we have to communicate so the person either understands immediately or is able to get clarification from us before the interview ends.

Reviewing Responsibilities

Sometimes when you tell how the information will be used, the person you're interviewing is so moved to play a part that he or she will launch this final section of the ending, telling what he or she will do or asking what you'd like him or her to do. Other times, you make the move, using your planned ending.

Whichever way the interview moves ahead to this final part, always say first what you will do (e.g., "I'll read this and ...") and then what the other person will do. Putting your part first shows your commitment. Even if what you're going to do chronologically comes after what he or she is going to do, go first: for example, say, "When I get your written information, I'll make notes and call you with the outcome" rather than starting with "When you give me your written information ...."

Be sure to suggest that the person take notes on what each of you will be responsible for doing. Then show your notes and have him or her compare the two sets of notes out loud. This assures both of you that you have the same understanding and saying it again can only help to reinforce the message and the commitment.

Actually say the words "Thank you for...." So often we forget this. We're rushing at the end and we figure that, since we've emphasized the facial expressions, gestures, and tone of voice that say, "Thank you for all the information" throughout the interview, the person knows we appreciate his or her time and the information. Say it anyway. It's unlikely that you'll have said it so often in the interview that it doesn't sound sincere!

Your last words should be a paraphrase of what you'll do and what the other person will do next: e.g., "I'll call you next Wednesday," "I'll talk with your references when you have them call," "You'll call me to assure me your broken ... is fixed." There should be no questions or doubts about what each of you is responsible for doing now.

Manager's Checklist for Chapter 6

❑ The most important parts of the interview are the beginning and the ending. The primacy-recency effect shows us that people remember the first and the last things we say or do.

❑ Be prepared for unexpected beginnings. Take care of the issue and then use your interview beginning from your interview planning tools.

❑ Use the Communication Style First Communication matrix and the Reason for Interviewing First Communication matrix to determine the order in which you conduct the beginning of the interview based on the person's communication style and the reason for the interview.

❑ No matter how rushed, follow your interview plan to the end. The ending is crucial to achieving your feeling objective and information objectives in the future.

❑ Reiterate the responsibilities of each person after the interview. You should state them, both of you should write them and go over them, and then you should paraphrase them as you thank the person for the information he or she gave you.

What Are They Saying ... and Conveying?

Since we are born with two ears and one mouth, we should listen twice as much as we speak!

Do you spend more time talking than listening when you interview? Interviewing experts say that the most effective and efficient interviews are those in which the interviewer talks *only 25% of the time!*

This makes sense: the more you talk, the less time you have to gain information from the person you're interviewing. You need to talk some of the time, of course, so the person will know the objectives, learn about your organization and you so he or she feels comfortable to give you information, and understand what information you need.

However, interviewers often go beyond what's necessary. Why do we talk so much when we're trying to get information from others? Here are a half-dozen reasons:

- We didn't plan sufficiently, so we talk while we're thinking of the next question.
- We're nervous.

- We're so excited about our organization and what we're doing that we give more information than necessary.
- Our communication style makes us naturally less succinct than others.
- We usually talk only 25% of the time, but more if the person is boring or difficult to get information from.
- We've learned that talking a lot is good in interviewing.

No matter what the reasons for talking more, we should aim at the 25% mark. Some things we've learned already will help:

- The open-ended questions we ask will cause the person to talk more.
- Behavioral questions focus on the person's experiences, so he or she will feel comfortable and talk more.
- The planning process and our interview tools with objectives written at the top will help us to stay on track.

In this chapter we'll learn active listening skills that will further help us limit our talking to 25% of the time.

Simply having a percentage target made a huge difference for me, an Expressive who's naturally less than succinct. I now plan for 25% and then keep track of the time. For example, if the interview is planned for 30 minutes, I plan for about seven minutes of talking—and I pay attention to the clock during the interview.

Taking notes in your Interview Planning and Conducting Tool will help, too, as it's more difficult to talk and write at the same time—although, if you do, you'll likely say less in that time and probably less coherently.

Notice that none of the ideas above are just to be a *better listener*. They are all action items we can do overcome our tendency to talk more than the person from whom we're trying to gain information.

Active Listening

Active listening shows you're interested in what the person has to say so he or she will say more. If people have labeled you a poor listener, active listening techniques are for you!

> **Active listening** A way of paying attention to what other
> people are saying and how that can make them feel that you
> are understanding them. It's essential to effective interviewing.
> Active listening shows interest through certain behaviors, including body
> language, facial expressions, paraphrasing, asking questions, giving feed-
> back, and taking notes.

We begin to unlock our ability to use active listening behaviors with the 10 Keys to Effective Listening.

Key	The Ineffective Listener	The Effective Listener
1. Find areas of interest.	Tunes out dry subjects.	Asks himself/herself, "What's in it for me?"
2. Focus on content more than delivery.	Tunes out if delivery is poor; uses preset ideas of why people act in certain ways to assign meaning to the way they deliver.	Avoids jumping to conclusions about the meaning of the poor delivery.
3. Hold your fire.	Tends to enter into arguments.	Defers judging until he/she understands completely.
4. Listen for ideas.	Focuses on facts.	Listens for central themes.
5. Be flexible.	Looks flustered or even acts angry when unexpected things occur. Can't make mid-course corrections.	Thinks on his/her feet and creates a calm atmosphere when there are distractions or unexpected events or actions.
6. Work at listening.	Shows limited energy output.	Works hard to exhibit active body state.
7. Resist distractions.	Allows distractions.	Plans ahead to avoid distractions. Tolerates bad habits. Knows how to concentrate.
8. Exercise your mind.	Takes information as it comes; sticks with what he/she knows.	Uses challenging material as exercise for the mind.

Figure 7-1. Ten keys to effective listening (continued on next page)

Key	The Ineffective Listener	The Effective Listener
9. Keep your mind open.	Reacts to emotional words; quick to judge.	Interprets emotional words while resisting getting hung up on them; considers possibilities.
10. Capitalize on the fact that thought is faster than speech so use the time constructively.	Tends to daydream with slow speakers.	Anticipates, summarizes, and weighs the evidence.

Figure 7-1. continued

What Are You Listening For?

In your interview tools, you've planned what specifically to look for and hear in the interview that would tell you that you were getting the information you needed. You'll have more complete information to use to make decisions if you know what you're listening for and use active listening behaviors to get it.

Listen for body language, facial expressions, voice tone, and pacing as well as words. Note in your interview tools what you see and hear. Avoid jumping to conclusions about the meaning when the delivery is poor—hesitations, lack of eye contact, too much information, etc. Later, when you're using the information you gathered, you'll have more information than if you'd drawn conclusions about what you observed.

It's no wonder so few people consider themselves "great" at interviewing. It's a juggling act that requires excellent focus and concentration. At the same time, you also have numerous other responsibilities, projects, things you're concerned about.... It'll be easier for you to listen for all the things you need to know when you have a general understanding of what you'll see and hear.

Listening for Body Language and Facial Expressions

Movements of mouth, brow, and eyes (pursed lips, smile, mouth open, clenched teeth, furrowed brow, raised brow, indirect or

Record Now, Interpret Later

Remember to write in your interview tools what you see and hear. Just record—as opposed to drawing any conclusions. Take advantage of the fact that thought is faster than speech: anticipate, summarize, and weigh evidence to develop questions based on what you see and hear the person "saying." Instead of interpreting the evidence in just one single way based on generalizations about behavior, think of the evidence in terms of *revealing possibilities* not *providing proof.* Keep in mind that behaviors may differ from culture to culture and from individual to individual and according to the situation.

varying eye contact) are the most obvious behaviors, the easiest to note. Write what you see as you're writing the words the person is saying.

Look for body position and for the type and amount of gestures. Is the person sitting up straight, crossed arms, leaning on something? Does she talk with her hands or hold them in her lap or play with objects? Does his body face you directly or sideways? Write down what you observe and later you'll have a context for a more accurate picture of what the person was communicating.

When you see something that concerns you (I know, you're not assigning one meaning, but it did concern you), you'll need to get clarification on it. Look for:

- If a person averts her gaze for a long time and/or at times other than when visualizing an event, it may mean she's

Beware of Generalizations

There are books that tell us how to read body language. These may be valuable in general, especially if they make us more aware of the importance of body language. But a little knowledge can be a very dangerous thing, since these books can cause us to jump to conclusions in interviewing. With that in mind, you may benefit from reading *How to Read a Person Like a Book* by Gerald I. Nierenberg and Henry H. Calero (Metro Books, 2002) and *Teach Yourself Body Language* by Gordon R. Wainwright (McGraw-Hill/NTC Publishing Group, 2002, new edition).

not telling you the truth. (See Chapter 8 for ideas on what to do to get the truth.)

- If a person crosses his arms frequently, it may reveal a desire to protect himself. He may be nervous, unsure of himself in this situation or in general.
- If a person is resting her head on her hands or leaning on the table, it may mean she's bored or not taking this inter view seriously. In a performance interview, for example, it may mean that the employee disagrees with you.

> **⚠ CAUTION!**
> **Read the Eyes Cautiously**
> A person will usually break eye contact for a second or two while visualizing an event associated with your questions. After a pause, he or she will either give you a description or ask a question for clarification. This break of eye contact and pausing is a normal part of the thinking process, not a sign that there's something that you should explore.

- If a person is fidgeting, it may mean he's nervous or he's avoiding telling you the truth. In an interview with a customer, for example, it may be that he or she doesn't want to give you the whole picture of what happened.

Listening for Tone of Voice, Pauses, and Pacing

Get into the habit of listening carefully to the tone of voice people use. Again, as with body language and facial expressions, you want to avoid making any judgment of what it means. Just note it and write it down with the words. Then consider what it could mean and ask questions to clarify.

Here are some examples of things you'll hear that you ought to explore:

- Nervous or false laughter, if combined with an averted gaze, is likely to indicate that the person isn't telling the truth.
- Nervous or false laughter, when combined with asymmetrically furrowed brows, is likely to indicate that the person thinks you're not telling the truth or is at least skeptical.

For example, a potential customer might react this way while making a comment after listening to your ideas about how your product/service meets his needs.

- Pauses longer than a second or two may signify that the person is distracted by a concern about being caught telling you something that's not the whole truth or is trying to remember a previous untruth.
- Talking fast may mean the person is nervous or, if you haven't noticed other signs of nervousness, is getting through an uncomfortable lie or repeating a rehearsed answer. You might hear this from a vendor or a consultant, for example, when you ask about a particular policy of theirs.

Listening for Specific Words

In your interview tools, you've listed some specific words you're looking for the person to say and/or words you don't want the person to say and you're so used to taking notes on words that this should be easy, right? My problem is getting stuck, placing so much meaning on the words I don't want to hear that I miss other words. Having the words listed in my interview tool to check off certainly helps. Having an idea of words or word categories that might be problematic enough to cause me to ask questions gives some things to focus on in general:

- "hopefully," "possibly," "maybe": These words may reveal a lack of confidence, either in what the person is communicating with that specific sentence or in general. They certainly don't instill confidence in the listener: for example, a vendor who says, "Hopefully you have more information about our services than you did before I came" doesn't make me feel very confident!
- "you must," "you have to": These words, especially in any interview situation, tell me that the person is awfully sure of himself or herself. This might be great if it's a vendor telling me what we have to do to be in compliance or fix a problem. This is not so great if I'm interviewing a current

> **⚠ CAUTION!**
> ### Maybe It's Just Style
> Remember what you know about communication styles from Chapter 2. Any of the problematic words may simply be typical of the person's style. For example, many very confident Amiables use the asking form when they need people to do something. Drivers are likely to say "you must"—but if you hear "you must" from an Amiable, it's cause for questioning.
>
> When you hear words that set off red flags, check first whether the words reflect the person's communication style. If not, then look for other evidence and ask questions.

employee or a candidate.

- "can you ...?" "could you ...?" "would you ...?" "why don't you ...?" "would you mind ...?" "do you think you might ..?": Some people use these "asking forms" regularly to mean that they need to know something or need you to do something (e.g., "Can I ask you if you have a telephone system that...?" rather than "Do you have a telephone system that...?" or "I need to know if you have a telephone system that...."). People who talk this way may be lacking confidence in what they're communicating now or in general. On the other hand, lots of people talk this way, thinking it's right and/or polite and not realizing that these structures suggest a lack of confidence.

You can do this—you can listen to words, watch the body and the face, listen to the voice, and write it all down. Practice

> Watch a movie or television show you've never seen (other than the news) for 10 minutes. Choose a character. For the first five minutes, just watch and listen. For the next five minutes, write what you see and what you hear.
>
> | Some of the Words | Body Language/Facial Expressions When Saying the Words | Voice Pace, Pause, Volume |
> |---|---|---|
> | | | |

Easy? Hard? Now, tomorrow watch another movie or show you've never seen. If you found the exercise challenging, do 10 minutes again. If you found it easy, do it this time for 15 minutes. Again, just watch and listen for the first five minutes, then listen and write for the next five or 10.

(Use a sheet of paper and make column headings as we did above.)

Did you notice any difference the second time? Was it easier? This is a skill. With practice, you become better at it and it becomes easier and, best of all, more automatic, which frees your brain for the other things that you'll be doing when you're listening during the interview. Keep practicing, either with movies and TV or in meetings.

---

and you'll see it's more natural than you might think. Try the exercise below.

Just how often do you need to practice to make it automatic? Research shows that we acquire habits in 21 days. So, if you practice every day for 21 days, it'll be automatic to listen and take notes while doing the other things you need to do in an interview. (If this sounds hard to believe, try this experiment. Move the wastebasket to the other side of your desk. It'll take about three weeks for you to stop throwing the paper on the floor!)

Active Listening Behaviors

We worked in Chapter 2 on our ability to recognize and modify to the person's most comfortable way of communicating. In Chapter 3 we worked on our ability to ask questions that engage the person we're interviewing and keep the interview flowing so it has a conversational feel. Our fluidity in an interview is important, because it keeps us in control: by asking the right questions we get the information we need and by creating a conversational flow and modifying to the person's communication style we create comfort that allows him or her to easily give us the information we need to meet our objectives.

Active listening skills will give you even more control over gaining the information you need to reach your objectives, as it allows you to take in all the information and it makes the person who's talking feel like we're listening so he or she keeps giving us information. Here are active listening behaviors you can CHEER about:

C Concentrate (Get rid of distractions and other barriers to listening so you can focus.)

H *Hear* totally (People communicate 7% through words, 38% through voice, and 55% through facial and body language.)

E *Empathize* (Think of a time you were in the same situation.)

E *Elicit* information (Ask questions and paraphrase.)

R *Remember* (Take notes in your interview tools.)

Hearing is distinctly different from listening. Most of us hear someone talking, but to listen involves using the active listening behaviors of CHEER.

Listening is a multisensory activity, using our ears, our eyes, and our senses of touch and smell to make the connection with the information stored in our brains about past experiences and our feelings about them. That's why the Chinese kanji for the verb "to listen" is composed of symbols for the eyes, heart, and attention as well as the ears.

> **Key Term**
>
> **Hearing** The physiological effect of sound waves resonating through the eardrum and other parts of the ear, producing an effect in the human brain that we call *sound*.
>
> **Listening** The conscious act of interpreting what those sound vibrations represent.

Active listening requires your conscious, active participation. It means being involved in the experience of what the other person is saying. Remember: successful listeners exhibit an active body state. This is really a good deal of work and so you'll do it only if you feel it's important for you to understand what the person is really communicating. Successful listeners have just as

"What's in It for Me?"

Mary is an unhappy customer. When she begins telling how our products "never" arrive when we say they're going to and she "always" has to call, it would be easy to show limited energy output. She's exaggerating and her accusing tone makes me less interested in working at listening to her. I'm a very precise person; I've been in Mary's situation, but I didn't react like she's doing so it's hard for me to understand.

If I ask myself, "What's in it for me?" I'd have to answer, "If I listen, I can find out what's really wrong, what's causing her to exaggerate this situation. If I can fix that and then not have to hear from Mary again, I'll have more time for other customers who don't exaggerate! Mary will feel better about us, Mary will have the product on time, Mary will say positive things about us, thus increasing sales."

I simply need to go through the quick process of asking myself, "What's in it for me?" I look at what I wrote in my interview tools as a reminder.

many other things on their mind as the rest of us; the people they interview are no different from the people you interview. The difference is that they've learned to empathize in every situation, to think of a time when they were in that situation or, if not, to ask, "What's in it for me?"

You'll be less successful with active listening behaviors if you're simply going through the motions. You need to be motivated. It will be difficult to take in all the information and make the person you're interviewing feel like you are listening unless you really want to get the information.

Ask yourself, "When have I been in a situation like the person I'm listening to?

If you can't think of any similar situation, ask, "What's in it for me? What are the objectives of this interview and what will achieving them do for me? What is this person's view of the situation? What is this person really trying to tell me?"

Maybe you start out motivated, but then begin losing interest in what the other person is communicating partway through the interview because of boredom or because you sense the person is exaggerating or not telling the truth. Remind yourself to do the following:

- Accept that what the person is saying is genuine, at least to him or her.
- Avoid interjecting your views, opinions, or solutions until the person has finished.
- Keep listening for the real message.

OK, so how do you *show* your interest through the CHEER active listening behaviors?

Many times it is easier to identify the behaviors that are exactly opposite of what we're trying to achieve.

When you've been talking and you thought the other person wasn't listening to you, what did you see him or her doing?

Now think of time when you felt the other person was really listening to you. List all the things the person did:

When finished, turn the page to compare your two lists with lists of common poor and active listening behaviors.

Body Language and Facial Expressions

Looking directly at the person, sitting or standing erect with open body posture, nodding, and using facial expressions appropriate for what the person is saying to you come more naturally to some of us than to others. Assuming you're motivated to listen, you may still not use all these behaviors—and, in fact, you may be able to listen quite well without some of them.

You may be one of those people who really can focus better if you're doodling. You may have your arms crossed in front of you because you're cold or because it's a habit for you and so it feels comfortable. You may be a Driver or an Analytical whose facial expressions don't vary much from one topic to another.

If any of these things are true about you, humor me for minute. Sure, maybe you can focus and take in information, but other people may not believe that you're really listening if they

Poor listening behaviors:
- interrupting
- look away from me when I was speaking
- doodling or fidgeting
- frowning
- sighing
- answering my questions with a question
- saying, "Really?" or "You're kidding?" or "No way!" when I described something
- finishing my sentences or paraphrasing incorrectly

Active listening behaviors:
- looking directly at me while I was talking
- taking notes (and looking up periodically and/or otherwise showing interest)
- sitting straight in their chair or standing (not leaning)
- open body language (arms and legs uncrossed, hands out of their pockets)
- asking me questions that related to what I was communicating (and not for information they already had)
- paraphrasing what I'd said
- nodding periodically
- saying, "Uh-huh," "Yes," or other forms of verbal nodding (but not robotically)
- a facial expression appropriate to what I was saying

judge by your body language and facial expressions. What happens when people don't think we're listening? They either go on and on since they don't get a signal from us that we understand or start giving very short answers or even stop giving information altogether! You may be able to listen with your arms crossed or while looking out the window, but you won't get as much coherent information if the person is spending part of his or her thought process wondering why you're not listening.

If you're buying what I'm selling, you're now saying, "OK, so I want people to feel comfortable and feel like I'm listening, but I've been doing it the other way a long time." (Remember: we're not talking here about behaviors that reveal because we're not motivated to listen. If that's the case, go back a few pages and

TRICKS OF THE TRADE
"To See Ourselves as Others See Us"
Maybe you don't know what you look like while listening and so you aren't sure if you need to change anything. (After all, how many people watch themselves in a full-length mirror while they're listening?) Ask someone who has talked to you extensively to tell you exactly what you were doing with your face and body the last time he or she talked with you. Then, if you need to make some changes, use whatever approach has helped you in the past to change any other habit:

* Replace one behavior at a time with the new one.
* Have a "coach" tell you when you're doing what you want and when you're doing something else.
* Use a mirror.
* Use a video camera.

find a way to be motivated.) So, your behaviors are just a habit. Well, the way to make new habits is—yes! you didn't even have to look it up: do the new thing for 21 days and, voilà, new habit!

Using active listening body language and facial expressions will cause the person who's talking to feel like you're listening and thus give more information and be more comfortable doing it. And, for the vast majority of us, these body states will heighten our ability to concentrate, to focus even when the other person is boring or just goes on and on.

Now that you've added active listening body language to your skill set, try that television, movie, or meeting practice from several pages earlier in this chapter. With active listening body language, you'll find it's even easier to take in the information.

Paraphrasing

Think of a recent time when you described a problem to someone and you felt like the person really understood your problem. How did you know? It's likely he or she paraphrased—rephrased and condensed what you'd said. Paraphrasing is incredible for clarifying and for showing that you're listening to the person who's communicating. (I keep using the word "communicating," since the words and the voice convey only 45% of the message.)

How does it feel when the person who is listening to you

paraphrases? Most people express the following reactions:

- "The person understands me."
- "The person is listening."
- "What I said is useful, is important."
- "The person will take action."

How does it feel for the person who paraphrases? Most people who are able to paraphrase say they feel like:

- "I can move forward confidently."
- "I have the information they need."
- "I have good rapport with the other person."

I like to feel the way both the person being paraphrased and the person paraphrasing feel, so I'm going to paraphrase. The actual act of paraphrasing, condensing, or rewording what the person was communicating to you is simple. What's hard is listening to a lot of information (verbal and non-verbal) so you can paraphrase. Assume you're motivated to listen and assume you're using the active body postures and facial expressions—both of which make it easier to focus.

> ### Paraphrase, Don't Parrot
> **Smart Managing**
> Use paraphrasing when a message is about a very involved problem or contains a lot of information about one thing. Using paraphrasing for short messages—a person says, "I didn't receive the coupons you said you'd send" and you say, "So, you didn't receive the coupons"—is not only a waste of time but it may sound like parroting instead of paraphrasing and actually irritate the person you're interviewing.

What trips me up every time is that, while the person is communicating, particularly a message that's involved enough that it would be useful to paraphrase, using the active listening body posture and facial expressions doesn't stop me from doing what's natural to most busy people—if there's a problem, I want to solve it, or if the person is giving me information, I want to go on to the next piece of information I need.

So, naturally, when I offer a solution, it may be wrong,

because I didn't listen closely enough to the problem, or when I ask a question, it'll feel choppy, because I didn't listen to the end and make an appropriate transition or because the person gave me some of the information I want but I missed it while getting ready to talk.

What should you do to avoid this natural mistake?

When someone is describing a problem or giving a lot of information about something, you need to focus consciously on the communication for the sole purpose of paraphrasing successfully. To help maintain your focus on taking information, take notes in your interviewing tools, because it's difficult to solve problems or get ready to talk while you're taking notes!

Paraphrasing will not only help you understand and make the person feel like you're listening, thus encouraging him or her to give you *more* information, it will help you get *less* information when that's what you want.

You want less information when you're interviewing a candidate for employment and the person is entering into areas where information could cause potential legal difficulties for you. You want less information when the person is going on and on and you think you understand what he or she is trying to communicate.

Paraphrasing works in both cases because it tells the person you understand and the two of you can move on. We'll work on the specifics of using paraphrasing for getting *less* information in Chapter 8 (pp. 158-159).

Paraphrasing is a great way to show and/or tell the person what you understood so he or she is less likely to feel a need to repeat or elaborate. And, if your understanding is incomplete or inaccurate, the person can clarify now.

Asking Questions and Giving Feedback

Asking questions is another great active listening behavior. In addition to getting you the information or clarification you need, questions that relate to what the person is communicating encourage him or her by showing you're listening, much like paraphrasing. Writing what they're communicating (words, body/face, voice) in your interview tools allows you to see pieces of information that aren't clear or complete. It's crucial to use what you learned in Chapter 3 to construct your questions.

> **Go with the Flow**
> Avoid asking questions for no purpose other than to show that you're listening. If the person is providing information you want and if you're understanding, then you're succeeding—so why interrupt the flow?
>
> **Smart Managing**

What if you really don't need to ask any clarifying questions? What if the person you're interviewing is an expert communicator and answers every question very specifically? How do you keep the interview from sounding and feeling choppy?

Another way to provide feedback is by acknowledging with verbal responses—"Uh-huh," "Yes," or other forms of verbal nodding. You should do this periodically; it's especially effective when you also nod your head or express with your face an emotion that's appropriate to what the person is communicating (a smile, a look of concern, etc.). You can also comment on what the person has said. Be careful to wait until he or she has completed the whole thought before you interject your views, opinions, or solutions. This will make it feel like feedback, rather than an interruption, like you've been listening, not just figuring out what you wanted to say.

Taking Notes Using Your Interview Tools

Taking notes using your interviewing tools does three things for your ability to reach your objectives through active listening:

- When you're taking notes, it causes the person to feel you're listening, so he or she gives you more information.
- When you're taking notes, it's easier to avoid jumping to conclusions because of the way the person delivers the information and to keep from reacting emotionally to what he or she communicates.
- When you're taking notes using your interviewing tools, any concerns you have about how it looks to be using

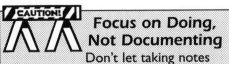

Focus on Doing, Not Documenting
Don't let taking notes become more important than taking care of the interview or you'll have less to take notes on (and you know why too!). If this becomes a problem, just take down the key points during the interview and then take five minutes immediately after the interview to jot down details.

your tools while you're interviewing diminish: the person feels great that you're taking notes and the papers become either welcome or not very noticeable.

Most people who interview are most concerned about writing *too much*, which will cause them to be looking down too much, or writing *too little* because they're so into the conversation and forget until later, when they can't remember much! Both problems will make it difficult to maintain a conversational flow, be concise and therefore timely, and make decisions based on the information that they didn't get or can't remember. By constructing the tools to make it easier to take notes (see Chapter 5, pp. 96-100), you'll be able to stay more focused on the person you're interviewing.

Getting Rid of Barriers to Listening

It's as crucial to identify any barriers to listening actively as it is to identify a motivation to use active listening behaviors. We've already dealt with some of the difficulties:

- "I get stuck on the words I don't want to hear them say and I miss other words." See pp. 137-139 for ways to get rid of this barrier to listening.
- "I'm comfortable. My non-active listening body postures are habits." See pp. 142-144.
- "I'm busy solving or getting ready to ask the next question so I miss out on information and I don't paraphrase or ask clarifying questions enough." See pp. 145-146.

Here are some more potential barriers and ways to avoid them.

The danger of the interviewing tools is that they give us some very specific things to listen for and can easily cause us to miss other information. To minimize that danger, keep this in mind: effective listeners listen for central themes; they focus on the main message. Write the individual pieces of information you're seeking in your prepared interview tools and write other information on a blank sheet of paper. (If you're interviewing candidates for employment, see the section in Chapter 5 on legal issues.) Paraphrase every so often to see how these other pieces of information relate to the information you set out to gain.

"I don't agree or I feel or even know that they're not telling me the truth." Listen with the intent to understand. Strive to listen from the person's point of view. Even if you disagree, accept that what the person is saying is genuine—at least to him or her. Write it in your interviewing tool, since writing makes it more difficult to make value judgments. (Remember the right-brain functions and left-brain functions from Chapter 6?)

"The person used words that are emotional triggers for me." We may be bothered by repetitive filler words or phrases, such as "um," "you know," "like," and "OK?" The first step to overcoming this barrier is to know your emotional trigger words. Then, let your direct employees and your peers know which words bother you and ask them to avoid using those triggers. When interviewing outsiders, you'll need to determine to set your emotional reactions aside—no matter how the triggers might upset you. The very process of identifying and listing your triggers makes it easier to deal with them. Those triggers have greater emotional power when they catch us by surprise. When you've written them, it's like planning for them. I know the words that will set me off and make it difficult for me to listen objectively, so I can plan to set my emotional reactions aside.

"I have a hard time focusing on what people are saying when they're so nervous and they're fidgeting or they have a scratchy voice or other poor communication behaviors." Poor communication in an interview situation may or may not signify issues later. Be concerned about delivery if you're interviewing a candidate or a volunteer for a position where verbal delivery is crucial or a consultant who'll be facilitating training or group work. On the other hand, if you're interviewing customers or peers or (in some cases) direct employees, avoid letting poor pronunciation, poor grammar, too fast or too slow rate of speech, dialects, fidgeting, and other factors distract you and interfere with your listening. Asking people to repeat things you didn't understand is a great active listening behavior. Focus on the words: write them down and write the voice, even if it's bothering you. Put less emphasis on the delivery. (This is exactly opposite what we advised in the "What Are You Listening For?" section of this chapter, but it's necessary to reduce any possible bias when interviewing people who speak differently than you just because of their experiences, attitudes, beliefs, and values, as discussed in Chapter 2.)

"When constructing my interview tools in Chapter 4, I planned the environment and planned out all the distractions I could. But what about the unexpected?" Make a list of all the ones you can think of that you can't plan for, such as coughing, sneezing, hiccupping, needing a bathroom break, really loud thunderstorms, and fire alarms. (We'll deal with distractions that come from interviewing with technology in Chapter 9.) Consider all sources: you, the other person, people outside the interview, and events.

The listing makes you aware of the possibility of a range of distractions, so it feels almost as though you've planned for them. If any of the listed distractions occur, you'll be ready.

If the distraction is caused by you, by other people, or by events, comment on it—just the facts, not your feelings about it—and apologize. Then, if you can do anything to stop it, do so or ask someone else to do so. If the distraction is caused by the person you're interviewing, acknowledge it by offering your help ("Are you OK?" or "Do you need a break or a glass of water?"). Don't mention the distraction ("You're coughing, would you like

Allow for Gender and Cultural Differences

Be careful not to judge all people by the same expectations. Gender and cultural differences can lead you to misin-
terpret what you hear and see if you aren't aware of them. Here are
some examples:

- Men's voices are generally deeper and their bodies are often bigger,
  so they may appear authoritarian or confident than they actually
  are.
- Women tend to ask more questions, which may make them seem
  hesitant or uncertain.
- People from outside North America may avoid eye contact to show
  respect; it's not necessarily a sign that they lack confidence or
  they're being less than honest.

And this is the tiniest snapshot of all the communication differences
that may seem significant but are just a matter of gender and cultural
differences. I'd recommend reading *Mars and Venus in the Workplace: A
Practical Guide for Improving Communication and Getting Results at Work*
by John Gray (New York: HarperCollins, 2001) and *Intercultural
Competence: Interpersonal Communication Across Cultures* by Myron W.
Lustig and Jolene Koester (Boston: Addison-Wesley, 1998, 3rd edition).

a glass of water?"); some people will be embarrassed by what's
happening and if you put it into words it may make them even
more uncomfortable.

In either case, once the distraction is over, simply paraphrase the last statement, whether it was your or theirs. It
immediately brings the focus back.

We can certainly be distracted when people don't act as we
expect. In Chapter 6 we dealt with unexpected actions at the
beginning of an interview. In Chapter 8 we'll work on the causes
of some of those unexpected actions and responses that will
allow you to reach your objectives.

Manager's Checklist for Chapter 7

❏ Plan to talk no more than 25% of the time.

❏ Know the general things you're listening for in body language, facial expressions, tone of voice, and words, but

8

What if They Don't Act Like I Expect?

We must look for the opportunity in every difficulty instead of being paralysed at the thought of the difficulty in every opportunity.

We've all interviewed "difficult" people, right? *Wrong!* We've interviewed people who've exhibited "difficult" behaviors.

Our ability to gain the information we need and meet our feeling objective when someone is acting in a way we didn't expect, in a difficult way, depends on our ability to separate *personality characteristics* from *behaviors*.

Ask yourself the following questions:

1. Can you change someone's personality? ___ yes ___ no
2. Can you change someone's lifelong attitudes and values? ___ yes ___ no
3. Can you change someone's motivational needs? ___ yes ___ no

The answer to all three questions is *no!*

You can't change someone's personality. *You* can't change someone's attitudes. *You* can't change what motivated someone.

What you can change, though, is how *you* act and react in a way that causes people to change their behavior. When people behave in a way that's different from what we expect, it's rarely something we label as good. We regularly label it as bad, wrong, or difficult and attribute it to the person (personality) rather than to what the person is doing at that moment (behavior).

The first thing you need to do is change your *language*. Use language that focuses on the *behavior*, not the *person*, and you'll find you're focusing on the behavior!

TRICKS OF THE TRADE

Focus on the Behavior, Not the Person

Start using *behavior* words instead of *personality* words. For example:
- Say, "This person is giving me too much information" instead of "This person is too talkative."
- Say, "This person is not telling the truth" instead of "This person is a liar."

Next you need to know the *cause*, why the person is acting differently than you expected. How you'll handle behavior that's different than you expect differs greatly depending on whether it's someone who's different from you or someone who's just acting different. Is the person using too few words because his or her culture has taught that it's a sign of respect when talking with a superior? Is the person being vague because the language differences between the two of you didn't allow him or her to be sure of your meaning? Know if the behavior is caused by different beliefs, attitudes, and/or values (see Chapter 2, pp. 39-43), as opposed to causes that are changeable (your actions, the person's nervousness and/or poor communication skills). We'll learn later in this section that an effective way to help someone act less vague is to use paraphrasing to pull together what he or she has said and then get the specifics with additional questions. If the person's language is different from yours, using more of your language to help him or her get more specific is only going to increase the discomfort and vagueness. If the person is vague because of poor communication skills, paraphrasing will help you get the information.

Learn the cause of the behavior and then you can choose responses that will help the person change that behavior.

Six Difficult Behaviors

The following are the six most common behaviors that make it difficult to get the information we need:

Vague—lots of words, little substance. The vendor described their services thus: "We provide mobile Internet solutions for institutions and mobile operators. We make m-business happen globally by powering secure mobile transactions across a wide range of Internet-enabled devices. Our focus is on two core verticals—we can enable your services and mobile networks to extend their services through the mobile Internet by deploying and integrating personalized and secure mobile commerce and lifestyle applications that will provide you with immediate new revenue sources and operational efficiencies."

This is not about whether you understand the language. The vendor simply used too many words that didn't relate to a specific objective—or maybe to anything at all!

Superficial—lots of words, no substance. Reaching the end of the interview, the manager asked the candidate for employment (a recent college grad), "What starting salary were you looking for?" The candidate said, "In the neighborhood of $125,000 per year, depending on the benefits package." The interviewer said, "Well, what would you say to a package of five-week vacation, 14 paid holidays, full medical and dental?" The candidate sat up straight and said, "Wow, are you kidding?" The interviewer said, "Yes, but you started it!"

Superficial interviews often are full of fun and humor. Fun and humor are important elements for keeping the conversational quality of an interview, but when you're halfway through the interview time and you haven't been able to write anything in your Interview Planning and Conducting Tool, you know you're not achieving your information objective.

Too much information—lots of words, too much substance.
We started the three-hour strategic planning session with a
recap of last year. Our peer in charge of a complex area of the
business handed out a 40-page report describing last year's
progress. After one hour of the person reading from the report
and expounding on each point, we were only on page 3.

In some cases, like this one, the volume of information may
be necessary for understanding. But if it's presented in a time
frame that's too short for the volume, it will overwhelm people
for whom the information is new. In other cases, you may be
getting more information than you need.

Too little information—too few words, little substance. When
the customer in a problem-solving interview was asked to
describe the experience he'd had with the service, he simply
said, "I don't like it when people hassle me."

Unless your question was closed-ended, you'd always
expect the answer to be more than eight words. Also, of course,
the words weren't specific enough for you to know what the
customer was talking about.

Avoiding the truth—substance is questionable. You asked your
direct employee in a performance coaching interview to tell you
each of the actions he took while working on a project that was
way behind schedule. He got right to the point and gave you
very specific information about what the other two project
members did to slow down the project.

You will certainly interview people who do not tell you the
truth, but it's far more common for people to avoid the truth.
When you ask a question about what the person did (since
you're using behavioral interviewing techniques) and the person
answers with what others did or did not do, you're dealing with
someone who's avoiding the truth.

**Anger—lots of words or too few words, substance is exagger-
ated.** You're interviewing a potential customer to determine her
needs for your products and she says, "The last salesperson
told me that we'd have the product ready to use a week from

the sale date and it not only wasn't ready but it didn't work and no one would call me back and my bill was huge. Well, I never paid it and now they're calling me everyday! People in your industry just aren't trustworthy!"

Anger is easy to spot and hard to handle. Some people go on and on when they're angry (like Expressives) and others (Drivers and some Analyticals) say even fewer words than usual in an effort to keep from losing control. The anger will always cause exaggeration, because of left brain/right brain functioning. We learned in Chapter 6 that the right half of the brain houses emotion and the left half of the brain houses reason, logic, facts. When a person is angry, the communication between the right and left halves of the brain is cut off. The person is stuck in right-brain thinking (emotion) and unable to do left-brain thinking (reason, logic), so he or she will be less specific and will exaggerate.

Behaviors, Possible Causes, and Your Response

Of course you can prevent many of these behaviors by using the planning and preparing techniques from Chapters 4 and 5! But what do you do if you just can't prevent a behavior?

Remember your information and feeling objectives for the interview. As uncomfortable, irritating, and frustrating as some of these behaviors are, you need to dispense with them tactfully and quickly so you can get the information you need and generate the feeling you want.

Most of the people you interview will not be acting in these ways intentionally, to make you uncomfortable, irritated or frustrated—though there are certainly times when it feels like it's intentional! Knowing what's causing the behavior is crucial to determining the response that'll get you back on track quickly

Here are the six behaviors described above, some possible causes for them, and some basic responses. In a few pages we'll work on how you can figure out the specific cause for this person in this situation and the skills needed for responding.

Vague—lots of words, little substance
Possible causes:
- Poor communicator
- Doesn't have the information or didn't prepare enough to have it

Your response:
- Ask specific questions by beginning with a paraphrase of what the person said. (Active listening behaviors encourage poor communicators and people who aren't prepared.)

Superficial—lots of words, no substance
Possible causes:
- In a hurry
- Likes to talk
- Expressive communication style
- Doesn't have the information

Your response:
- Paraphrase what the person said and ask another of the specific questions you planned.
- If the cause is that the person just doesn't have the information to meet your objectives, thank him or her for whatever information was given and end the interview.
- If the cause is that the person is in a hurry, comment on it and reschedule or take a minute to plan for what you can cover in the time he or she has.
- If the cause is communication style, see Chapter 2, "Recognizing Communication Styles and Modifying to Adapt."

Too much information—lots of words, too much substance
Possible causes:
- Poor ability to organize the information
- Analytical or Amiable communication style

Your response:
- Paraphrase as soon as you have the information you

need, to confirm that you understand. Following your Interview Planning and Conducting Tool will also help if the person has problems organizing, because your organization will help him or her.

- Stop the person from giving you information that will cause legal issues with "don't need to know" information (see Chapter 5). Say, "I want to keep us on track with the information relating to ..." and then restate your question or ask the next. Or say that you know the person is busy and wants to keep to the time. In this situation only, never, never, never paraphrase what the person said that you didn't need to know.
- If there truly is a lot of information, have the person give you as much of it as possible in writing before the interview, as part of the preparation.
- If the cause is communication style, see Chapter 2, "Recognizing Communication Styles and Modifying to Adapt."

Too little information—too few words, little substance
Possible causes:
- Nervous
- Not telling the truth
- Doesn't have the information or didn't prepare enough to give you information
- Doesn't think he or she has the information

Your response:
- Paraphrase what the person said and ask another of the specific questions you planned or use a different type of question to get the same information (Chapter 3).
- If the cause is not telling the truth, see below.

Avoiding the truth—substance is questionable
Possible causes:
- Afraid the outcome of the interview won't be favorable if he or she tells the truth
- Protecting someone else

Your response:
- Accept that what the person is saying is genuine, at least to him or her. Look for a pause and jump in. Letting the person go on avoiding the truth will only make it more uncomfortable when the truth comes out. The less chance you allow him or her to tell things that are untrue, the more likely you can get the truth and then continue the interview amicably.
- Listen for the real message and paraphrase as though that is what the person said.
- If the person's method of avoiding the truth is to tell what others did, paraphrase and then restate the original question. (If you just restate the question or say, "I don't want to hear what others did," you'll be dealing with a person who's avoiding the truth—and is now angry.)

Anger—lots of words or too few words, substance is exaggerated
Possible causes:
- Not telling the truth, so angry with himself or herself
- Being treated in an accusatory manner or talked down to
- Having to wait longer than expected
- Being lied to
- Personal issues

Your response:
- Let the person vent. Never tell him or her to calm down.
- Use active listening: that behavior will keep the person talking and some of the words he or she uses will help you figure out what the person is trying to tell you.
- Match the person's intensity. (Anger is just negative excitement, so be excited in a more positive tone of voice and body language. If you act calm, it'll look like this isn't important to you and the person will get angrier.)
- Ask questions. Remember that the person will have trouble at first answering anything fact-based since he or she doesn't have access to the left brain. Ask with no question

mark (rising inflection tends to fan the flames) and use the person's communication style (e.g., for a Driver, "We can be more productive if I know....").

Other Causes

I'm sure you noticed that none of the six causes listed were "purposefully misleading" or "enjoy being hard to deal with" or "lay awake in bed last night figuring out how to make your life miserable." The percentage of people whose behavior is motivated by any of these causes is extremely small. Actually, the cause of difficult behaviors is generally our beliefs about the people and our resulting actions.

A traveler was walking toward a village and on the road he met another person. The traveler asked, "What are the people like in the village up ahead?" The other person said, "What were the people like in the village you just came from?" The traveler said, "Oh, they were rude, selfish, and boring." "Well," said the person on the road, "that's just what you'll find in the village ahead." The traveler said, "Of course," and then walked off in a different direction.

A little while later, another traveler came upon the same person on the same road. He asked, "What are the people like in the village up ahead?" The person on the road asked, "What were the people like in the village you just came from?" "They were just delightful, so friendly, always wanting to help each other and so interesting to talk with!" "Well," said the person on the road, "that's exactly what you'll find in the village up ahead."

Our response affects the behaviors of the people we interview. The second traveler will interview very few people who act difficult on purpose. The second traveler believes that the people he interviews want to give the information; it's just that something is making it difficult for them. So he'll use responses that help people give information in the interview no matter what's causing the difficulty. He knows that the cause of difficult behavior is different for each person and each situation. He'll figure out the cause so he can use that knowledge to help choose the response that will make it easy for that person to

Be the Second Traveler

• Show understanding of the causes for the other person's behavior.
• Find positive connection with the other person.
• State contentious points in positive form.
• Maintain a positive and cooperative attitude.
• Be open to discussing negative comments and criticisms.
• Be open to suggestions and solutions from the other person.
• Work toward a win-win situation.
• End on a positive note.

give the information he needs.

The responses listed in the sidebar are based on some general skills for helping people give you the information you want when their behaviors are making it difficult. Use these responses as your starting point, then learn the general skills presented later in this chapter and use them to modify your response to fit the specific situations.

The causes listed above are a starting point. In the next section we'll learn how to figure out the causes for each person and each situation.

Figuring Out the Causes

You're asking questions and the person is giving you vague answers. Now, in addition to asking questions, setting up other methods, listening actively, and writing in your Interviewing Planning and Conducting Tool, you're thinking about the causes so you can choose your response. Whew!

Figuring out the cause of the vagueness is crucial to choosing the response that will help the person provide information that meets your objectives. Take a quick break, if necessary, so you can get some uninterrupted brain time—go down the hall to get something to show the person, ask if he or she needs a drink refill, get one for yourself. A few seconds of downtime will make a big difference in your thinking ability.

Whether you think on the spot or take a quick brain break, thinking on yet another level in an interview is not easy. Before you put any time into figuring out the cause for behavior that's different than you expected, gage the person's willingness and ability to change his or her behavior—to be more specific, to become less angry, to give less information, etc. Plot the person you're interviewing on the Willing and Able Chart (Figure 8-1).

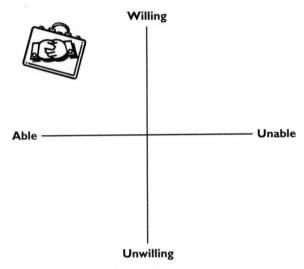

Figure 8-1. The Willing and Able Chart

Let's use Ted the Talker as an example.

Does Ted seem *willing* but *unable* to give less information? Is he talking rapidly and does he sound excited and positive? If so, then using the responses above, or others you determine fit him, will work. Paraphrase as soon as you have the information you need, to confirm that you understand. Follow your Interview Planning and Conducting Tool to help Ted organize, if that's the cause. Help him keep on track. If he talks a lot because his communication style is Analytical or Amiable, try the suggestions in Chapter 2 for the appropriate style.

Does Ted seem *unwilling* but *able* to give less information? Have you seen him in other parts of the interview or in other situations get to the point and give less information? If so, and if you want to proceed with the interview, you'll need to stop, identify the reason he's unwilling (the tactics for avoiding the truth apply here), and remove it. If you can't, you can either end the interview or go forward and expect that it'll take longer to achieve your information objective. It's also unlikely in this environment that you'll be able to achieve your feeling objective.

Does Ted seem both *unwilling* and *unable* to give less information? If so, then even if you can determine the reason he's unwilling, if you can't do something to improve his ability to give less information, the interview will take longer and you'll get information you don't need to know. Move forward with this person only if the information must come from him (e.g., an employee's performance appraisal or a customer with a problem).

Does Ted seem both *willing* and *able* to give less information? Is he obviously excited to tell you all the things he's telling you and he's been more to the point at other times in the interview? If so, then it'll be easy to help him give you only the information you need.

Repetitive why analysis A method of probing for the root cause of a situation by asking "Why?" over and over until you determine one underlying factor that seems to be most fundamental, the basic cause in the chain. This technique is similar to the *five why's* approach used in the quality movement.

OK, now you've plotted the person on the Willing and Able Chart and you've decided to go forward based on your analysis of their willingness and ability. To gather the information you need to uncover the *real* cause of actions you didn't expect, use *repetitive why analysis*.

Use repetitive why analysis to identify:

- Hard data—facts, results, events, history, statistics, forces, goals, procedures, physical phenomena, observable deviations, time factors, trends, productivity, quality and performance levels
- Soft data—feelings, opinions, human factors, frictions, attitudes, satisfaction levels, stresses, frustrations, personality conflicts, behaviors, hearsay, intuition, "gut" reactions, mental blocks

In most interviews you'll be asking yourself the "why" questions, as opposed to asking them of others. For example, imagine asking Ted, "Why are you giving me too much information?" He may not even realize he's doing that, so asking this question will sound antagonistic. The purpose of repetitive why analysis is to gather data so you can understand the cause of the behavior and determine the best response. So instead of antagonizing Ted, ask yourself, "Why is Ted giving me too much information?"

Is It You?

The first "why?" should always be directed toward examining our own actions.

It may be that what's causing Ted to give you too much information is that you're unable to ask specific questions or that you didn't modify to his communication style so he's struggling to understand what you want. If Martha is giving you too little information, it could be that she senses irritation in your voice. If Sandra is angry, it could be because you seem unprepared for the interview. If Andrew is avoiding the truth, it could be because your questions seem aggressive, challenging.

I am always happy when the cause of a difficult behavior is my actions, because I can change them. We have ideas in this chapter and Chapter 6 for actions you can take to help people change their behavior. Try as you may, you are you and they are they and only they can change their actions. On the other hand, when I'm the cause of Ted giving too much information, I have total control (I'm not saying it's easy to change) over my ability to improve my skills so I get only the information I need.

When the person you're interviewing exhibits difficult behavior, look at your actions first. Ask yourself what you're doing right now that's causing that behavior or contributing to it and make changes on your feet. After the interview, as you should after all interviews (see Chapter 10), look at skill changes you'll need to make to be more effective in future interviews.

Is It ...?

Let's say it's not you. You've done everything right—or at least

you've done enough things right that it appears you didn't contribute to the behavior that you didn't expect. Ask yourself,
"Why besides something I'm doing is Ted giving me too much
information?"

You've noticed that Ted has been twisting the paper clips on
your desk throughout the interview, so he may be nervous. You
could stop right there and say, "Aha, Ted's nervous and that's
why he's giving too much information. I must do something about
his nervousness." But what will you do? You could implement the
ideas for helping people feel less nervous. This is a great strategy—if the real cause of the behavior is the nervousness. But, just
for fun, before concluding that nervousness is the cause, ask
yourself, "Why is he nervous?"

He told you that he had another appointment at 1:30 and
it's getting close to that time. Aha, the cause for him giving too
much information is that he's concerned about the time and so
he isn't as focused as he was earlier in the interview. Alleviate
his nervousness by letting him know that you know: "Ted, it's
1:15 and I know you need to leave in about five minutes. One
last question—What did you do about...?"

When he knows you're aware of the time and his need to
leave soon, he can focus on answering your specific question
instead of being distracted by concerns—"I have to leave. Do
you know what time is? Do you remember that I have to leave?
What should I do?"

If you'd stopped asking "Why?" when you realized he was
nervous, you'd have tried to do something about his nervousness, which would not have helped him. On the other hand, if
you ask "Why?" too many times, you risk losing your focus on
interacting with the person you're interviewing. This will cause
another whole set of problems.

Repetitive why analysis on your feet is not an easy or perfect technique. But it will give you more information than you
had before, which can only help you deal with the situation.

Now, you're asking yourself the why question and answering
it, again and again, and trying to decide when you've asked and

answered enough times to be sure you have the real cause and then taking action, all while you're conducting the interview. Whew! It helps me to have made a big list of possible causes, so I'm not thinking from a blank brain!

What's Behind the Behaviors?

Which behavior is the person exhibiting? What do you think the reasons are?

Behavior You See	Possible Reasons for That Behavior
❑ Short temper ❑ Arguing ❑ Critical of others ❑ Abrupt ❑ Speaking loudly/shouting ❑ Complaining ❑ Too much information ❑ Angry ❑ Vague ❑ Too little information ❑ Sleepy ❑ Fearful ❑ Crying ❑ Poor work performance ❑ Superficial ❑ Add others from your own experience _____	❑ Frustrated with job duties ❑ Frustrated with a person ❑ Problem at home ❑ Problem with coworker ❑ Bad hair day ❑ Problem with boss ❑ Problem with customer/client ❑ Ate too much at lunch ❑ Tight deadline ❑ Resentment ❑ Being counseled for perform- ance ❑ Tired because _____ ❑ Angry about _____ ❑ Wrong job for the person ❑ The person's previous supervi- sor created poor productivity/ lack of consistency/fear. ❑ You spoke negatively to the person in front of others.

Figure out the cause and your response will fit the situation. Responses that fit the person and the situation are more likely to create a change in the person's behavior.

Your Response

We have some ideas for responses to the most common difficult interview behaviors (pp.157-162). How you implement those responses is crucial to turning around a difficult situation so you can get the information you need. It's one thing to say that if the person is avoiding the truth, you're going to "accept that what the person is saying is genuine, at least to him or her, and look for a pause and jump in." It's a whole other thing to do it without communicating irritation that the person is not telling the truth!

Communicating your responses assertively helps you get your message to the person in a confident but not demanding or demeaning manner. Assertive communication gets people to listen to what you need them to do differently!

Assertive, Passive, or Aggressive?

There are three ways you can communicate messages— assertively, passively, or aggressively. Most people recognize *passive* communication, but many get confused between *assertive* and *aggressive*. Here are the words people use to describe each of these ways of communicating messages:

Passive	Assertive	Aggressive
quiet	confident	controlling
following the crowd	in control	loud
holding back	knowledgeable	conceited
meek	open	brusque
lacking confidence	skillful	curt
shy	good-natured	intimidating
wimpy	flexible	"my way or the high-
	concise	way"
	determined	angry

Which list of words would you like to have people using about you? "Assertive" looks best to me. So why doesn't everybody communicate assertively? For some it's lack of skill; for others it's lack of knowledge. Some of us think we're communicating in a confident, in-control manner in an interview—and are surprised when the person reacts to us negatively. There's a fine line between "confident" and "conceited," between "in control" and "controlling." You may *act* assertively but people may not always perceive it as such. And we all know that perception is reality! But you need to start by actually communicating assertively. How assertive are you? Do the assessment activity in this box.

You Can't Fake Assertiveness

In how many situations are you acting assertively right now? Read each statement and rate yourself from 1 ("I never do this") to 5 ("I always do this"):

_____ I ask others to do things without feeling guilty or anxious.

_____ When someone asks me to do something I don't want to do, I say "no" without feeling guilty or anxious.

_____ I am comfortable when talking with a group of people.

_____ I express my honest opinions to others, including my boss.

_____ When I experience powerful feelings (anger, frustration, disappointment, etc.), I verbalize them easily and appropriately.

_____ When I express anger, I do so without blaming others for "making me mad."

_____ If I disagree with the majority opinion in a meeting, I can "stick to my guns" without feeling uncomfortable or being abrasive.

_____ When I make a mistake, I will acknowledge it.

_____ I tell others when their behavior creates a problem for me.

_____ Meeting new people is something I do with ease and comfort.

_____ When discussing my beliefs, I do so without labeling the opinions of others as "crazy," "stupid," "ridiculous," or "irrational."

_____ I assume that most people are competent and trustworthy and do not have difficulty dealing with others.

_____ When considering doing something I have never done, I feel confident I can learn to do it.

_____ I believe my needs are as important as those of others.

Scoring: Total your points and divide by 14.

The closer your score is to 5, the more often you act assertively. Look at the statements for which you gave yourself less than 4. Work on one or two of these to start acting assertively in general more often.

Acting assertively in all situations will make it second nature, so it will be easier to do it in an interview.

Some of us are anxious about communicating assertively

because of the number of times people have perceived us as communicating aggressively. But anxiety undermines confidence—and lack of confidence comes across as passive (or even aggressive, as we try to compensate by pumping ourselves up).

You remember from Chapter 3 that how a person understands us is based 55% on facial expressions and body language, 38% on voice, and 7% on our words. It's more likely that the person you're interviewing will perceive your communication as assertive if you use body language, facial expressions, and voice that have been described as assertive:

55% facial expressions and body language
- Look the person in the eye. (If you don't, you're perceived as aggressive—"too good to bother with me"—or passive—"too nervous to look at me.")
- Use open body language. Unfold your arms, keep your hands apart and out of your pockets, uncross your legs.
- If you "talk" with your hands, keep the movements flowing, rather than choppy.
- Your facial expressions should be calm (not deadpan, but not intense or surprised).
- Stand up. (It's almost impossible to be perceived as assertive while sitting.) If the other person is sitting and you can't get him or her to stand, sit straight up in your chair without leaning back.

38% voice
- Keep your tone of voice firm. (If you're concerned about shaking, lower the pitch of your voice and speak more slowly, so your voice can't crack or shake.)
- Keep your volume even—not too loud (aggressive), not too soft (passive).

7% words
- Paraphrase the person's words.
- Avoid negative words (such as "no," "I can't," "it's impossible," "but," "it's not good," and "however").

- Avoid words or phrases that are seen as passive (such as "hopefully," "possibly," "maybe," "kinda," "sorta," "only," "just," "I guess," "can you ...?" "could you ...?" "would you ...?" "why don't you ...?" "would you mind ...?" and "do you think you might ...?").
- Give options, alternatives, or specific things for the person to do (e.g., "...and I specifically need to know the number of times the product didn't work").

How you think you're communicating and how someone perceives your communication may be different. Practice using in your everyday communication the body language, facial expressions, voice, and words that are perceived as assertive. Then you'll be ready when it's crucial to use them successfully.

There are times when I don't care if people perceive me as aggressive. In fact, I truly want to act that way, such as with candidates for employment whom I don't want to hire (so they don't want to work here) and vendors who are wasting my time (so they stop calling me). Whatever you do, resist this temptation. Even though communicating aggressively may get rid of these people, it may also get rid of terrific candidates, terrific vendors, and even current employees and customers—because these people have friends, these people are potential customers! Always put your best face forward for the sake of your organization and yourself!

Avoiding Negative Emotions

When you allow someone's behavior to make you impatient, irritated, or angry, you'll be stuck in your right brain, where you'll have access only to emotions, exaggeration, and creativity but not to facts, reasoning, and logic. All your careful planning and all your wonderful "difficult interview behavior" skills will be inaccessible. You'll be less able to recognize and modify to the person's communication style. Your ability to ask questions using the voice and body language you planned and to use active listening skills will be greatly impaired. Your body

Plan to Avoid Upsets

To avoid human and job sacrifices to Murphy's Law, the best insurance is a little contingency planning. What things might upset you, so you can't keep calm enough to use your great "difficult interview behavior" skills? The obstacles can be obvious or hidden. Your planning for any interview should include thinking of all the things that could happen and the way you'd act if someone acts in a way that's different from your expectations:
- What could go wrong?
- What can I do to prevent it from happening?
- If it happens anyway, what can I do to fix it?

language, your facial expressions, and your voice will likely convey the impression that you're not listening. When you don't look like you're listening, the person gives you less and less information. As for your ability to come across assertively, ... well, have you ever see an assertive angry person?

The times we most need to come across as assertive are the very times it's most difficult. Sometimes it's simply that some aspect of the person immediately turns us off and then it doesn't take much for us to feel that he or she is being difficult. It's easy to say you'll think from a detached point of view, watch out for making assumptions about people, and stay focused on the Interview Planning and Conducting Tool, so you'll be able to get the information that you need. Just like it's easy to say you'll use the responses suggested in this chapter or that you'll always use the assertiveness skills.

The best defense is a strong offense, so prepare to stay calm by taking the following steps:

- Keep your "conflict storage" empty. Issues that you don't resolve can cause you to get impatient or angry at the least provocation. Take action on conflicts as they come up, instead of holding onto them. Maybe you think you can just let go of things—but if someone behaves in a difficult way, do you immediately think about other things that aren't going well? If so, then deal with conflicts and problems as soon as possible.

- Keep it professional, not personal. One way to do this is to try to use "organization" words such as "the company" or "we" and "us" instead of "I" and "me."
- Remember that you're in control when you remain calm. It may feel like the person who's being difficult is in control because the behavior makes you uncomfortable, even intimidated, but whoever remains calm is really in control. (The person who gets upset is locked in his or her right brain. If you get upset, too, both of you will be locked in your right brains—and two rights make a wrong!)
- Maintain your positive attitude no matter what happens. Use those positive assertiveness words: success comes in *cans*, not *can'ts*. Think the positive outcome first. If the person is yelling; say to yourself, "That's great: I can practice staying calm" or "That's great: if I use active listening skills, I'm sure there's some information here that I need." That works better than saying, "I hate when people act like this" or "I can tolerate it."

You have an incredible amount of influence over the outcome of interview situations in which the person acts differently than you expect. Make your attitude "negative-proof," plan

Attitude

Smart Managing

"The longer I live, the more I realize the impact of attitude in life. Attitude, to me, is more important than facts. It is more important than the past, than education, than money, than circumstances, than failures, than successes, than what other people think or say or do. It is more important than appearance, giftedness, or skill. It will make or break a company, ... a church, ... a home.

"The remarkable thing is we have a choice every day regarding the attitude we will embrace for the day. We cannot change our past ... we cannot change the fact that people will act in a certain way. We cannot change the inevitable. The only thing we can do is to play on the one string we have and that is our attitude.

"I am convinced that life is 10% what happens to us and 90% how we react to it."

—Charles R. Swindoll

so you're less likely to cause difficult behavior, and use your skills for determining the causes of the behavior. This will allow you to choose and implement the response that'll get the interview back on track for getting the information you need.

Manager's Checklist for Chapter 8

❑ We can't change the person we're interviewing, but we can change how *we* act and react in a way that causes the person to change his or her behavior.

❑ Focus on the *behavior* instead of the *person*.

❑ Look for causes so you can determine your best response to difficult behavior.

❑ Find the real causes by using repetitive why analysis.

❑ Use facial expressions, body language, voice, and words that cause people to perceive you as communicating assertively.

❑ Keep yourself from getting angry or irritated so you'll feel in control of the interview and be able to get the information you need.

How Do I Use Technology Successfully?

What was the best thing before *sliced bread?*

Technology can be an incredibly useful tool. Or, it can be just a cool thing replacing traditional, face-to-face interviewing but making it more difficult to gain the information you need. Choose it to help you, not because it's cool.

There's a whole host of computerized and telephone screening software programs for candidates for employment. There are software programs for discovering customers' needs. You can build a section of your Web site to get information from customers who need help with a product or service. You can also simply gain the information you need from a candidate, direct employee, customer, or colleague by e-mail, telephone, webcast, or videotape.

Just because these tools exist—and more are being developed every day—doesn't mean we need to use them. Your job is to gain the information you need in the fastest, most accurate manner.

> **Sometimes Face-to-Face Is the Only Way** ⚠️CAUTION!
> Interview in person when:
> * It's a complicated or sensitive issue (e.g., direct employee with an interpersonal communication problem)
> * The people involved are uncomfortable with using technology tools for an interview
> * The people involved need to interact with the product or service (e.g., operating a piece of equipment)
> If you must use a technology tool in any of these situations, because of geographical distances and transportation time and expense, be sure to acknowledge and remove or minimize the obstacles for the person before the interview or at the beginning.

In the previous chapters, we learned all the things we need to do to gain that information. Use that knowledge and the tips in this chapter to make decisions on when using technology will be beneficial to your particular situation. Avoid "boldly going where no man has gone before" just because it's fun or someone asks you to.

What's Different When Conducting Interviews Using Technology?

The benefits and the drawbacks center around three major differences between using technology and in-person interviewing:

* Real time vs. delayed time (synchronous vs. asynchronous)
* Ability to see the person vs. inability to see the person
* Verbal vs. written

In-person interviewing creates a situation that is real time, verbal, and visual. These three aspects give you the most conversational feeling and the most information, as you have the 55% body language and facial expression and the 38% tone/volume of voice along with the 7% words. (See Chapter 7.) Using technology tools for part or all of the interview creates obstacles, as you have the opposite of one, two, or all three of these important aspects. Even when you have all three, as you do in a videoconference or a webcast with telephone support, you have the obstacle inherent in technology—it simply may not be functioning right now! The list below shows each type of technology according to the dimensions mentioned above:

- Real time—telephone, instant messaging, videoconference, conference call
- Delayed time—e-mail, videotape, audiotape, computer-assisted
- Ability to see the person—videoconference, videotape
- Inability to see the person—telephone, instant messaging without webcam, e-mail, audiotape, conference calls, computer-assisted
- Verbal—telephone, videoconference, conference call, videotape, audiotape, webcast with telephone support
- Written—e-mail, instant messaging, webcast without telephone support, computer-assisted

There are absolutely benefits to using technology tools for part or all of the interview. The fact that there are obstacles as you lose one, two, or all three of the optimal aspects for gaining the information you need shouldn't scare you away. Obstacles are those frightful things that take your eyes off your goals. Keep your eyes on your goals, choose the technology that benefits your situation, and know the obstacles so you can remove them.

The table beginning below tells you how to decide when and what technology tool to use.

Tool	Benefits
Telephone/ Teleconference	Interviewee unable to travel because of time or cost, need real time to build rapport, you need to hear his/her reactions.
Videoconference	Interviewee unable to travel because of time or cost, interviewee needs to see demo, you need to see his/her reactions, you need to hear his/her reactions, information too complex or detailed for verbal communication, need real time to build rapport.

Tool	Benefit
Webcast with telephone support	Interviewee unable to travel because of time or cost, interviewee needs to see demo, information too complex or detailed for verbal communication, need real time to build rapport, you need to hear his/her reactions.
Instant messaging	Interviewee unable to travel because of time or cost, information too complex or detailed for verbal communication, need real time to build rapport, gives written documentation.
Webcast without telephone support	Interviewee unable to travel because of time or cost, interviewee needs to see demo, information too complex or detailed for verbal communication, need real time to build rapport, gives written documentation.
Videotape	Interviewee unable to travel because of time or cost, you need to see his/her reactions, you need to hear his/her reactions, you and interviewee need time to gather, organize, and revise info before giving, interviewee needs to give info based on his/her schedule only.
Audiotape	Interviewee unable to travel because of time or cost, you need to hear his/her reactions, you and interviewee need time to gather, organize, and revise info before giving, interviewee needs to give info based on his/her schedule only.
E-mail	Interviewee unable to travel because of time or cost, information too complex or detailed for verbal communication, gives written documentation, you and interviewee need time to gather, organize, and revise info before giving, interviewee needs to give info based on his/her schedule only.

Tool	Benefit
Computer-assisted	Interviewee unable to travel because of time or cost, information too complex or detailed for verbal communication, gives written documentation, you and interviewee need time to gather, organize, and revise info before giving, interviewee needs to give info based on his/her schedule only.

Telephone, Conference Calls, and Videoconferencing

Real time and verbal—two out of three of the optimal conditions! The telephone, either one-to-one or a conference call, is the most effective technology tool to use in an interview. Everyone is used to giving information on the phone, it's inexpensive, it requires no special setup, and, since it's real time and verbal, it comes close to in-person interviewing.

You can make that three out of three of the optimal conditions if you use videoconferencing, since you'll be able to see the person. Using videoconferencing to interview one person or a group is the closest you'll get to doing it in person. It takes a special setup and not everyone is used to this type of conversation, so to be effective it'll take a bit more planning than the other telephonic methods.

Using Interview Technology at Nike

Nike's Retail Division uses a combination of technology tools in interviewing candidates for employment for its stores. They start with a telephone prescreen. The successful candidates then participate in a computer-assisted assessment in the store that includes watching a video and interacting in a role-play. The final step in the information-gathering process is an in-person interview.

This process has saved an enormous amount of time for store managers and it's been really well received by the candidates. Why? Because of the initial collaborative planning and ongoing feedback. Planning and feedback center around:
- capitalizing on the benefits of technology
- setting up and maintaining the tools
- overcoming the obstacles to using the tools

Setup

You'll of course use your Interview Planning and Conducting Tool (Chapter 5) to plan the timing, the specific information to gather, and the method. Use the following list to help you set up for the technology.

Timing. Remember when setting the time that people may be in different time zones. To avoid confusion, always state the time in your zone (10 a.m. EST or 3:30 p.m. MDT) and let each person calculate the difference for his or her zone.

Determine Who Initiates the Call. For telephone or videoconferencing, it could be either you or the person you're interviewing, since you both have to have the equipment/service. Decide which based on the reason for the interview:

- candidates for employment/volunteer—have them call you to show timeliness
- direct employees—you call them to show how important their development is to you
- peers—the person who's in charge of the project should be the initiator
- current and potential customers—you call them to show how important their needs are to you
- vendors and consultants—you may want them to call you to show timeliness and how important your needs are to them
- colleagues—it's a coin toss

For teleconferences, it depends on whether you or the people you're interviewing own the service or you're using a service provider. If you own the service, it's obvious that you'll be initiating. If you're using a provider, most offer both services where you initiate and services where you give each person a number to call to get into the teleconference. Choose based on the above recommendations. (Note: the pricing may differ for the two types of service.)

Communicate Who Initiates Call. Do you want to guarantee a late start? All you have to do is be unclear about who's initiating.

Give Instructions in Writing. You can get instructions for receiving or getting into teleconferences or videoconferences from your equipment or service provider.

Give Tips in Writing for Communicating in Teleconferences/ Videoconferences. Even people who have used these methods to give information will benefit. You can greatly reduce the obstacles, as very few people have had any training.

The following box contains tips you can give to people who will participate in the teleconference.

Tips for a Successful Teleconference

A teleconference is a telephone call with several people. Just as with one person on the phone, you lose the communication that comes from face and body. In addition, with more than two people, it requires special techniques to get any person to talk and to keep more than one from talking at the same time when you have no visual cues.

✔ Your voice and your words carry your communication. But you can't lean back in your chair, feet up, and make ugly faces, because your facial expressions and body language come out in the tone, volume, and pacing of your voice. (Just try to sound upbeat and positive while scowling—it can't be done.) Use the same facial expressions and body language as if the others were able to see you. (Some people have used a mirror to help them with telephone facial expressions.)

✔ Expect pauses after you make a comment or answer a question. The others are taking notes.

✔ Expect the leader to ask for your input. The person has no visual cues whether or not you have a comment and is trying to include everyone.

✔ Reduce distractions. Since you're not talking the whole time, it's really easy to talk to another person, file, answer e-mail (and if you're on a mobile phone there's no limit on what you can be doing instead!). While you're doing these things, you're not using active listening skills and therefore not getting all the information. Sit or stand in a location that's quiet and free from other work.

Put papers away, face a wall, focus on the agenda and any other documents needed, post a sign that you're in a conference call, set all calls to go to voice mail, and turn off e-mail notification.

✔ Murphy's Law: someone else will call when it's time for your appointment. End the call as quickly as you can and use someone else's phone to check your voice mail to see if you missed the person calling you.

✔ Start each comment by identifying yourself.

Now, the following box gives you some tips for effectively leading a teleconference.

Tips for Leading a Teleconference

✔ Be in the teleconference five minutes before the start time and welcome each participant as he or she joins the teleconference. If you're initiating, begin early, allowing yourself one minute to join each person.

✔ Facilitate introductions as people join; then they can be talking and building rapport while waiting for the interview to begin.

✔ Review the Tips for a Successful Teleconference as part of the methods part of the interview.

✔ You'll need to actually ask people to answer questions. Without visual cues from you or each other, you won't have the momentum that builds in in-person group interviews. The first few times you interview by teleconference, it'll feel to you like the people aren't interested, since you're used to people participating without a lot of prompting. I assure you it feels much more uncomfortable to you than to them.

✔ People come in and out throughout the call—people come late or have to leave early or the technology dumps them out of the call. Most services announce that someone has joined or left. Determine whether you stop the current flow to acknowledge their entry depending on what you're talking about. This is no different from when a person joins an in-person interview. When someone leaves the teleconference without announcing it, just take a note, keep going, and call him or her later to gain the rest of the information.

✔ When you're taking notes, tell them so they don't wonder about the pauses.

And finally what follows in the next box are some technical tips for participants in a videoconference.

Tips for Participants in a Videoconference

✔ A videoconference is a telephone call with one or more people and you can all see each other! It requires special equipment and a service and some knowledge of how to use them.

✔ First, set your camera to output to the monitor so you see what the person on the other end of the call sees. Then you can adjust seating so all participants can be seen. Before the call, reset the monitor so you'll see your caller!

✔ Individual microphones provide the best sound quality. If you use a table mike, follow the manufacturer's instructions for optimal distance from the person who's talking. If there will be several people in the room, be sure to seat them so it's the optimal distance from all. It's a terrible distraction and an obstacle to the conversational flow if you have to keep moving the mike.

✔ Look at the person to whom you're talking, not at the video camera.

✔ Speak in a normal volume, as you would in person. If your microphone is set correctly, you'll be most successful using the active listening body language (see Chapter 7) and speaking in a conversational volume.

Capitalizing on the Benefits

On March 7, 1876, the U.S. Patent Office granted Alexander Graham Bell Patent No. 174,465 and the telephone was born. That technology allowed people to save travel time when they needed to get information from other people. We have Charles Ginsburg to thank for our ability to save travel time and see the person while we're talking. In 1956 he rolled out the first videotape recorder, which sold for $50,000. (They cost less now.)

So, with telephonic devices we can get information more easily and more completely from a distance. There's another benefit: we save time, because most people get to the point quicker when we interview by phone or videoconference.

The major obstacle to gaining information by telephone or teleconference—the loss of body language and facial expression information—also functions as a benefit, since we work extra hard to use our active listening skills because we must get 55% of the meaning by other means. I find myself more likely to be listening with the intent to understand instead of the intent to reply.

Web

Two effective ways to use the World Wide Web for interviewing are computer-assisted and webcast.

The webcast can be just like a videoconference, with both voice and video, using a microphone and a webcam. Or it can

Webcast Sending audio or video over the Web, the Internet equivalent of radio and TV broadcasting.

be viewing visuals created earlier or in real time in PowerPoint, Freelance, or any other software program, including ones that reside on your Desktop.

The interchange of written ideas can come from typing in real time or from a telephone call over the Web or on your telephone. You can use this technology when you're interviewing one person using NetMeeting, which comes bundled with Windows. For several people, you'll need a service: most conference calling services provide webcasting as well. To become familiar with how these services work, try all the above varieties at www.calleci.com.

With webcasting you can have all three of the optimal conditions (using webcam and the telephone), two of them (using the telephone while viewing the visual), or only one (typing

Computer-assisted interviewing A general term for using a computer in the interview process. CAI has been mainly used in computer-assisted telephone interviews (CATI), computer-assisted personal interviewing (CAPI), and computer-assisted survey information collection (CASIC).

back and forth to each other while viewing the visual).

Computer-assisted interviewing (CAI) ranges from forms the person fills out to multiple things to watch, read, and answer/fill out (much the same as very interactive

Web-based training). Either way, you create the tasks using Web authoring software or HTML, put it up on a Web site, tell the person how to access it, and then you'll later receive all of his or her answers, timing, questions, etc.

Use CAI when you need to gain information from many people, either all at once or over time. It's especially great for gaining information in the early stages of the interview—candidates for employment, potential customers letting you know their needs, and vendors and consultants submitting proposals. However, if you need group interaction or one-to-one interaction, as in performance appraisals and planning, and you need to use the Web, use webcasting.

Setup

The setup for webcasts is the same as for teleconference or videoconference (if you're using a webcam) above, plus just a few additions specific to using visuals. Use this checklist to help you set up for webcasts and computer-assisted interviewing.

Use the teleconference/videoconference checklist for webcasts.

Give Instructions in Advance and in the Methods Part of the Interview. This is in the previous checklist, but it's crucial to effectiveness so it bears repeating. If you'll be typing to each other instead of using voice, also use the checklist below for e-mail and instant messaging.

Using Visuals Without Being Able to Talk in Webcasts. You'll be typing to each other instead, so use the list on pages 187-190 for e-mail and instant messaging.

Technical Difficulties. Be sure that everyone has a phone number to call you if they can't get the Web page up or if they lose access to the Web altogether. If the problem is with the Web page, though everyone is used to problems with pages, it'll reflect poorly on you. For webcasts, choose a service provider whose current customers have had few difficulties and practice with the service *a lot* before you run your first webcast. (Most problems are operator errors!) For computer-assisted interviewing, have an expert create your forms, etc., and put them up on the Web (unless you're an expert and can do it yourself). When it works correctly, you'll save an incredible amount of time and get the information you need.

People Who Are Uncomfortable with This Technology. You will lose much information if the people don't feel they can participate. Know the people you'll be interviewing (Chapter 2) and, if they'll be uncomfortable, either use another technology (videoconference, e-mail) or have an additional alternate way for people to get you the information. Remember: the reason you choose Web-based interviewing is to get information from a lot of people, so you rarely have the option of training to help them get comfortable.

Capitalizing on the Benefits

Webcasting gives you the same travel time benefits as teleconference/videoconference and allows you to show visuals. (See Chapter 4 for use of visuals as a method in interviewing.)

For computer-assisted interviewing, you'll get automated correspondence for the future, because you'll have stored the person's e-mail address. You'll also save a large amount of people time for gaining information.

⚠ CAUTION!

Focus on the Fit

Computer-assisted interviewing saves time overall only if you can get the information you need asynchronously, without seeing or speaking with the person. Look at the *sensitivity* of the information. Will people want to give it to a computer screen? Look at the *complexity* of the information. Can the information be typed? Can the questions or other methods for gaining the information be implemented in a Web page? If the answer to any of these questions is no, you'll save people time up front but will have to do it all over using another technology or in person. Use computer-assisted interviewing when it fits the information and the people.

E-mail and Instant Messaging

E-mail and instant messaging are much less formal than other types of writing because of the immediate opportunities for feedback and clarification. Think of them as partway between writing a letter and talking. That means there are few hard-and-fast rules of style, which can cause communication misunderstandings. Add to that the loss of two out of three of the optimal conditions for instant messaging and three out of three for e-mail—and the results can be disastrous!

Never use e-mail or instant messaging for any sensitive communication, such as when a direct employee or a vendor has done something that doesn't please us or a customer is very angry or we made a really big mistake. That goes without saying, right? If you need to ask an employee to find employment elsewhere, do it in person or (as a last resort) by phone.

The speed with which e-mail in particular is replacing telephone calls makes it wise to develop our skills. I used to get 20-plus phone calls per day and now get two or three calls and 300-plus e-mails! Increasingly we are in some part of an interview (gaining information from another person) using e-mail even if we didn't plan this as the technology.

Many people communicate incredibly accurately and successfully using e-mail and instant messaging. Start saving e-mails that are easy to understand, just as you would save successful interview questions, brochures, etc.

Setup

Use the following list to help you set up for the technology.

Compose E-mails Off-Line if You Need to Reduce Connection Time. All you have in e-mail is your words and style; time pressure will make you less effective.

Wording Choices Are Crucial in Any Written Message. The 55% body language and facial expression and the 38% tone, volume, and pace of your voice—it's all in the words, 100% words! And you can't take them back. If you're using e-mail, have someone else read it to be sure it's the message you really mean to send. If you're using instant messaging, be prepared to explain a few things again—even the best e-writers aren't perfect.

Style and Clarity. E-mail and instant messaging are so informal we're likely to skip our usual writing style (grammar, spelling, punctuation). As those things go, so do completeness of thought and clarity. This sometimes means we don't finish sentences or we create run-on sentences. Your reader on screen, especially in instant messaging, is reading as though listening to you talk. So the stream-of-consciousness writing style (long sentences with hyphens, commas, and other means of being conversational) isn't wrong here. *But* (a big "but") once the reader prints out the e-mail or the transcript of the instant messaging session, voilà!— you now have a written letter and your style simply looks like poor grammar, spelling, and punctuation! Remember at all times that you are writing and, if in doubt, err on the side of the rules of informal written style.

Keep the Sentences and Paragraphs Short. Paragraphs, a novel concept! Cyberspace belongs to the short writer and "short" is as much about what they see as what they read. Breaking text into paragraphs and bulleted lists will give the feeling of short when you need to put a lot of words in your e-mail. In instant messaging, paragraphs will break up the look of the conversational stream-of-consciousness style.

Subject Line. Here's your chance to catch the attention of the recipient, especially if he or she receives a lot of e-mails. Keep it to 10 words or less, so the recipient can see most if not all of the words in the table-of-contents window, without opening the e-mail.

Signature and/or Electronic Business Card. This is a great way to provide more information about you and/or your organization without taking space in the body of the e-mail.

Use the Address They'd Recognize. Most of us have personal e-mail accounts in addition to our organization e-mail. When

Make E-mail More Effective

The shocking truth about e-mail ... is that some messages never arrive!

Sometimes we mistype an e-mail address, but the wrong address is viable, so we don't get an "undelivered" message back. Most e-mail software has a feature that requests that the recipient acknowledge receipt. Use it to be sure. (Note: The e-mail software may require the recipient to actually open the e-mail. A person who reads e-mail in a preview window will not know that you're requesting acknowledgment.)

Sometimes we do everything right and our e-mail arrives—but hours after we sent it, so the recipient doesn't recognize the subject line or our e-mail address or the recipient gets hundreds of messages a day and deletes by accident. Use your e-mail software to mark messages "urgent" and use the ideas above to make sure your subject line helps the recipient notice your e-mail.

The final truth is that some e-mails are just "out there"—and we'll never know why.

interviewing, use your organization account. When I travel, I need to use my travel account, so I purposely chose an address (trainingsys@netzero.com) that identifies my organization through the username, just as my organization address (cbt@trainingsys.com) identifies it in the domain.

Attachments. The recipient can open an attached file only if he or she has the program in which it was created. Ask in advance. If the recipient does not have the program, you have two options:

- Create a PDF (Portable Document Format) file. (Be sure he or she has Adobe Acrobat Reader.)
- Resave the file in a program you both have.
- Save the file as an RTF (Rich Text Format).

I like the PDF idea best, because all the formatting will be maintained and it's quick for you. If the recipient needs to do anything with the file besides read it or look at it, choose a software resave that keeps most of the formatting (or all of it if you send the fonts and tell how to load them). This will take more time than saving as RTF, as you'll likely be recreating some of the formatting if it doesn't survive the conversion.

Viruses. There are some nasty, dangerous viruses out there! To protect recipients and yourself, keep your virus-checking software completely up to date using the automatic update feature of your software and the most current version of your Web browser.

Capitalizing on the Benefits

We've talked a lot about the loss of meaning from facial expressions, body language, and voice, which may lead you to believe that writing is a more difficult, less accurate method of gaining information. In fact, in the more immediate world of e-mail and instant messaging, writing can serve to confirm understanding. Many times when we listen, we're doing so many other things we don't even realize we're not clear about the meaning of what we hear and see. Our filters (Chapter 7) are working automatically to determine the meaning while the person is talking. When we read, we're more likely to notice a word or phrase that may mean something different to the writer than to the reader. Why? Reading requires more of our attention than listening and we read at a rate that's closer to the rate at which we can take in and process information. The brain can process upwards of 600 wpm. Since people speak between 170 and 240 wpm, our brains are racing ahead and many times missing information. The average college student reads 250 to 300 wpm, a rate closer to the processing speed.

The written aspect of e-mail or instant messaging also has the following advantages:

- It is a source of documentation.
- It allows time to compose, organize, and revise ideas (e-mail only).
- It can be detailed.
- The recipient has some control over when to respond (e-mail only).
- It costs the least.

- We can take notes without being seen.
- It may reduce dishonesty, because it's generally harder for most people to write intentional lies for a permanent record.
- People may be more candid, because they can't see each other—which is great for employee exit interviews and customer reports on service/product quality.

Audio- and Videotaping

Audio- and videotaping are most likely to be used during interviews with current or potential customers to allow others later to get the full message (to see facial expressions and body language and hear voice tone, volume, and pacing). You can tape planning meetings or other activities so people who can't be present can see and hear what happened and feel more a part of the group and thus contribute information. Another use of video and audio is a pre-recorded tape. In an early part of the interview process, it can show skills, such as with a consultant who can display facilitation skills in a real situation.

Setup

Use the following checklist to help you set up for the technology.

Taping:

People Tend to Be Nervous. This is especially true of video, but also of audio. Be prepared for the first few minutes to be less than representative of the person.

Tell Them Ahead That You'll Be Taping. In most case you'll want to get them to sign an agreement.

Set the Taping Equipment in the Least Intrusive Location. See the checklist for videoconferencing.

Prerecorded:

Ask for Tapes of Exactly What You Need to See. Does it need to be a certain situation or in a certain location or from a certain time?

Tell Them What You'll Be Doing with the Tape After You Use It. Some people are concerned about sending tapes for fear of where the tapes could end up. Others may have had the tapes done professionally (at some expense) and it's a nice gesture to return the tapes if you don't need them, so they can use them again.

Capitalizing on the Benefits

It's so difficult to bring together every person you need at the same time. Taping is the next best thing to being present—far better than reading a written transcript or a report condensed with someone else's filters! In Chapter 4 and elsewhere, we've looked at time-saving methods of getting information before the interview or even to screen. Watching and/or listening to a tape is much more accurate than something you'd read if you're looking for information on a person's verbal communication skills or ability to complete a physical task or the way a piece of equipment or a service works. It's an underutilized screening method that I highly recommend, especially for determining customer needs and what vendors have to offer.

Manager's Checklist for Chapter 9

- ❏ Use technology because it will help you gain information in the most accurate and quickest manner, not because it's cool or someone asked you to.
- ❏ Choose the technology that fits your situation and know the obstacles so you can remove them or work around them.
- ❏ If it's a complicated or sensitive issue and you must use technology instead of interviewing in person, use a video-conference or webcast with videocam and telephone.
- ❏ Use your Interview Planning and Conducting Tool (Chapter 5) as usual, plus the checklists for each type of technology to set up the situation for effectiveness.

❏ The benefits and drawbacks of using technology center around these conditions: real time vs. delayed time, ability to see the person vs. inability to see the person, and verbal vs. written.

How Do I Use the Information I've Gathered?

When you get right down to the root of the meaning of the word 'succeed,' you find that it simply means to follow through.

—F.W. Nichol

After you've done all the preparation and gathered the information it seems hard to imagine that you wouldn't use it— but we've all done it at least once. And many of the obstacles have been the same.

Here are some possible obstacles to using the information and suggestions for overcoming them.

Another project came up. Compare the outcome for the project that came up and the outcome for the information gained in the interview. Which is more necessary to your organization? Can you do both by prioritizing or do you have to drop one? If the outcome for the interviewing information is to be dropped, keep the information anyway. You may be able to get back to using it and simply have to do a follow-up interview to update it. Or you may have to start again because the situation has changed: the

candidates for employment are no longer interested, the potential customers have gone elsewhere, the employee performance
difficulty is now a crisis, or the customer problem is worse.

**You just can't decide: it's hard for you to make important
decisions.** It's likely you're an Amiable or Analytical (Chapter
2). People of these two styles tend to take longer to make the
decision because they need to be sure it's the best decision.
Give yourself a deadline: tell the person you interviewed and/or
others involved and you'll be more likely to stick to it.

You don't have the information you need to make a decision.
It's possible you needed to spend more time planning with your
Interview Planning and Conducting Tool. Or you planned well,
but you weren't facile enough in asking the questions or listening or keeping up the conversational flow or dealing with difficulties getting information. Evaluate yourself and decide which
skill you need to improve (see pp. 207-210), go to the chapter
in the book that'll help you prepare, and then use one of the
methods for clarifying in the next section to get what you need.

**You found you needed more information and it seemed difficult
and/or time-consuming to get.** What's the obstacle to getting
it? How much time will it take to overcome the obstacle and get
the information? Is the outcome of using the information worth
investing that time? If so, figure out, alone or with others, how to
get the information and do your other work. Then use the methods for clarifying in the next section.

When you face any of these obstacles to using the information you gained, first assess the value of the time and energy
expended to remove the obstacle and then compare it with the
value of the outcome. Remember to think about the time you've
already spent that will have been wasted and the loss of goodwill, credibility, or even dollars if you don't use the information.
Look again at your objectives. How important is this information
and the result of using it to you and your organization?

What's common in all the obstacles is the need to spend additional time, either because we put off using the information or

because we discover we need a bit more information or we need to clarify some of our information. With our incredibly full schedules, prioritizing our time to meet the most important objectives will always be crucial to success. This feeling of lack of time can lead us to make decisions with the information we have. We're pretty sure it's clear and accurate, but not totally sure.

Methods for Clarifying When You Need Additional Information After the Interview

Clarifying information now will save you from fixing the problems that come from a bad decision.

Think of clarifying as a final method of gathering information. You may need only to get clarification on information from the person you interviewed or get information from an outsider. If it was a job interview, you probably (I sure hope so!) got information from someone else as part of the original interview methods (usually called "checking references"). Use the same outsider or other people to clarify. Whether clarifying with the person you interviewed or another person, remember to listen for the whole message, just as you did during the interview.

Something Just Doesn't Seem Right

In her job interview, Susan said she had supervised a staff of 10 field reps, but when you had her do an in-basket test, she couldn't understand an expense report. Either she was exaggerating her supervisory experience or she's not an effective supervisor. Which is it? Or is it just expense reports? Or maybe all financial reports?

Clarifying with the person you interviewed should feel like another opportunity for that person to give you information. If he or she sounds impatient or acts in any way that's inconsistent with the way he or she acted in the interview, you've just added information to help you make a decision.

Clarifying with the person you interviewed or with other people is part of gathering information. To be successful, use your Interview Planning and Conducting Tool to plan the beginning,

---

Discrepancy and an Attitude

You found an inconsistency in the information you wrote in the Interview Planning and Conducting Tool during a job interview. You call the candidate and tell him that you read in the booklet he gave you that the service lasts one year, but you wrote that he said it was two years, and you need to know which is accurate.

He tells you, in a rather huffy tone of voice, that it's one year and he didn't say two years. This gives you cause for concern and now you have to get clarification on that tone of voice.

---

the questions, and the ending, just as you did for the interview. In essence this is another interview, so with the clarifying method you choose use the same skills of asking questions, active listening, and working with people who don't act as you expect.

The following two tables help you decide what method to use to let the person know what you need to clarify and how you want him or her to give you the information.

If:	Method to Use
You need to hear his/her reaction to your message	Telephone or in person
It's a sensitive situation	Telephone or in person
It's a quick question that will also help create a positive feeling about you/your organization	Telephone or in person
It's a detailed question	E-mail
He/she needs to see a document quickly	E-mail
You're physically near each other	In person
You need to see something that can't be mailed, e-mailed, or faxed	In person

Table 10-1. How to let the person know what you need clarified

Situation	Method to Use
You need to hear his/her reaction	Verbally, in phone call or in person
It's a quick answer	Verbally in phone call or in person, send written answer/documentation by mail, e-mail, or fax
It's something he/she needs to look up or think about	Call back with answer, send written answer/documentation by mail, e-mail, or fax
Detailed answer	Send written answer/documentation by mail, e-mail, or fax
One or both need a record of providing the information	Send written answer/documentation by mail, e-mail, or fax

Table 10-2. How to have the person give you the information

Using the Two Tables

In his written performance appraisal, John said his greatest strength was his ability to perform well under pressure. You remember that during a plant emergency last month he got angry and wasn't able to apply an orderly thought process to solving the problem. Was that an unusual day? Is his definition of "ability to perform under pressure" that different from yours? Can he do some things well under pressure but not solve problems?

You need to clarify. This is a sensitive situation in which you need to see his reaction to your message and you're physically close so you go to John to clarify in person. This is something John will need to think about and for which you need to hear his reaction, so you'll be asking him to get back to you verbally. John is an Expressive.

Use your Interview Planning and Conducting Tool to plan out the beginning, the questions, and the ending and write an outline to follow on the back of one of the pages of your tool.

Beginning
- First Communication—"We'll be exchanging ideas about your greatest strength as listed in your performance appraisal, the ability to perform well under pressure."
- Our information objectives—(covered in First Communication)
- How much time we'll be together—15 minutes
- Methods for meeting our objectives—(covered in First Communication)
- Information about our organization and about us—(not needed in this case)
- His/Her objectives—"What other things do you want to cover?"

Questions
- "You described your greatest strength as the ability to perform well under pressure. In last month's plant emergency, you yelled at staff and it was an hour before you were working with them to use our standard problem-solving process. That to me was a pressure situation in which you needed to be able to apply the problem-solving process immediately. When you were thinking 'greatest strength: perform well under pressure,' what situation did you picture?" *Wait for his answer and then comment on whether you agree or not based on the situation he describes.*
- "Your ability to perform consistently well under pressure is important to your success. Over the next two days, think about these questions (*have him write them down*) and we'll meet on Friday to discuss them:
  - "What else was happening that day last month?"
  - "Make a list of the specific things you did well in the situations you pictured as examples of performing well under pressure."
  - "What times were you able to quickly use our problem-solving process?"

Ending

- What will happen with information after this clarifying—
  Talk about it if needed, then write it into his performance
  appraisal.
- Your responsibilities and his after—You will be available to
  talk Friday; he will think about questions and come with
  answers to the Friday appointment.
- Gaining commitment for what he'll do next—Watch for
  face/body agreement that he'll do it.

Making Decisions with the Information

You've planned, you've conducted, you've clarified, and
throughout the entire process you've taken clear notes in your
Interview Planning and Conducting Tool. All of these things,
along with the ideas at the beginning of this chapter, make it
easy to take the decision-making step. Over and over throughout this process, you've cautioned yourself to keep from jumping to conclusions. The time is finally (sigh of relief!) here to use
the information to make your decision.

What Are the Decisions You'll Be Making?

Candidates for Employment or Volunteer Work

Should we hire them? If not, should we consider them for another
position now or in the future? If so, what skill areas do we need to
pay attention to and help them develop in the beginning?

Your Direct Employees

Was their idea usable? When will it be used? Will they be asked to
find other employment? Will they move to another job or department? What skills do they need to develop? What are their goals?
Who will help them meet their goals? What methods will be used to
help them meet their goals? What is the problem? What methods will
be used to solve the problem?

Peers

Was their idea usable? When will be used? What are the goals?
What methods will be used to meet the goals? Who will be responsible for each? How will we measure achievement? What is the prob-

---

lem? What methods will we use to solve the problem? How do we prevent this from happening in the future?

Current and Potential Customers

What is the problem? What methods will we use to solve the problem? How do we prevent this from happening in the future? What do they need to be successful? How will we help them understand their need? How can they afford our product/service?

Vendors, Consultants, Colleagues

Should we use their products or services? If not, should we consider them for something in the future? Should we recommend them to other organizations? What is the problem? What methods will we use to solve the problem? How do we prevent this from happening in the future? How can we afford their services? Will we change our processes and/or policies to be like theirs?

The Interviewing Decision Worksheet (Figure 10-1) gives you a place to put all your possible decisions. Once you see them all together, written clearly right below the outcome, it's easy to determine which is the best decision.

Follow the instructions at the top of the worksheet and use all the information you gained and recorded in your Interviewing Planning and Conducting Tool(s).

Communicating the Decision and Creating a Positive Feeling About Your Organization

Ask any person who's given of his or her time and information, "What's the worst thing that can happen?" The answer is almost always "When I never hear what they did with the information."

You never hear whether you got the job. You never hear what your boss thought about the action plan you submitted for your development. You never hear why your ideas in the planning session haven't been implemented. You never hear what happened to your complaint. You never hear from the salesperson. (This one is always a mystery to me: you have money and the salesperson doesn't.) You never heard what happened to your proposal.

Interviewing Decision Worksheet
❑ Write at the top of the worksheet the SMART *outcome* for the situation.
❑ Write in the first column all the *possible decisions* (e.g., each candidate for employment, each solution to a problem, each method for achieving a plan goal).
❑ Look at your Interviewing Planning and Conducting Tool(s) (for candidates for employment and vendors, you may have more than one). In the second and third columns, write all the *potential benefits* and *potential risks/costs* (and specific examples from the information you gained for each) as they relate to the outcome.
❑ Mark in the fourth column the two *possible decisions* with the most benefits related to the *outcome*. The one of these two with the least *risks* is likely to be your *first choice* (i.e., the one that comes the closest to meeting the *outcome* without so many *risks* that it won't be worth it).
❑ Look at each of the *risks* for choice #1. Are these risks you can live with? If so, you've just identified your decision. If not, look at each of the *risks* for choice #2.
Your final decision will be the potential decision whose potential benefits identify it as coming closest to meeting the outcome with potential risk(s) you can live with!

Outcome:

Possible Decisions— Candidate/Vendor/ Solution/Method to Achieve Goal	Potential Benefits Related to the Outcome (example)	Potential Risks/Costs Related to the Outcome (example)	Choice #

Figure 10-1. Interviewing Decision Worksheet

Of course you believe that they chose someone or something else or made no decision. You wrestle with the idea of talking with them, but you don't want to seem a pest so you hold off. You feel bad that you or your ideas were rejected. You feel bad that you didn't try to talk with the person who inter-

> ## Deciding Right
> To make your decision making most successful:
> - Distinguish fact from opinion.
> - Verify the accuracy of your information by using multiple methods to gain the information.
> - Retain the sources of your information. (There are legal requirements for candidates for employment that range from one to two years, depending on the size of the employer and whether or not it's a federal contractor.)
> - Keep all variables constant (time of day, interviewers, objectives for the interview).
> - Identify variables you weren't able to keep constant and take into consideration.
> - Cross-reference the results of all the methods and look for consistencies and inconsistencies.
> - Make a decision! (There's a difference between being thorough and looking at "just one more thing, just one more thing....")

viewed you. You feel bad that he or she didn't care enough to contact you. In a word, you feel bad.

Rejection

How you communicate rejection of a candidate for employment/volunteer work or a vendor or consultant translates to how the person feels about you and your organization. You may decide not to work with that person, but you want to retain his or her goodwill (and that of his or her 1000 closest friends!).

You also want to keep the person from getting the idea that you didn't choose him or her for some discriminatory reason. (See Chapter 5, Legal Issues.) Most people assume they or their products or services are the best for the job. So if they don't get chosen and they don't know why, many assume it's because of something about them they can't help. Psychologically, it's easier for people to think that you didn't choose them because of their race or age than because of their skills and experiences or their products or services didn't meet your needs. It's human nature to want to know why. If you don't tell them, you leave it to their imagination and they may create reasons that don't cast a positive image of you and your organization. If you give them information, you may prevent them from coming up with reasons.

The same is true for your direct employees, your peers, your customers, and your potential customers when you don't decide in their favor after interviewing them. Whatever the purpose for interviewing them and whatever the outcome, you should communicate your decision.

People accept things more rationally and more comfortably when they at least know why. You know this matters to you, but when it comes time to do it for others you may hesitate. Why? And what can you do about it?

"I don't like to deliver bad news." Remember: it's *selection*, not *rejection*. Certain people, products, services, and ideas are right for a situation and others aren't. You're just selecting the one that gets you closest to your reason for gathering the information and has the most positive and least negative consequences. You're not rejecting the others. They may not see it now, but they or their products or services or ideas weren't the right fit and it wouldn't have worked out if we'd selected them.

"Our legal department told me not to give any information about why I decided against them." Use the description in this chapter of how people feel and their propensity to jump to conclusions to help convince your legal department to let you give specific information, prepared in advance (and approved by the legal department, if that's your bargaining chip). Make it specific to the skills required for the job or the specs or the product or service. This applies to candidates for employment/volunteer work (new to the organization), direct employees, vendors or consultants, and customers or potential customers.

"I'm concerned my 'I regret to inform you …' skills aren't good enough." It takes skill to keep that conversational feeling while being careful to give truthful feedback that's factual about the skills, the attributes of the product/service, the ideas as they relate to the job, spec sheet, company mission, or other criteria.

If you slide into generalities, you'll cause misunderstandings and possibly lawsuits.

You also want to avoid a debate—"But I do have those skills," "But my product does that," "But let me explain my idea further," and so forth. If you clarified, you're confident that they don't have the skills, etc. and trying to explain again to someone who's started down this road will only prolong the debate. Simply use the assertiveness formula (Chapter 8, pp. 168-171) to stick to your original statement.

"My policy is to give rejections only in writing." Many organizations have this policy because of the number of people who lack the skills of specificity you've now developed from working through this book! Practice, help others learn the skills, and then convince "the powers that be" that it would be better in the long run to have the individual conversation and follow it with a letter. A letter by itself is so cold. We use it to avoid hearing disappointment or anger over the phone. Instead, the person expresses that disappointment or anger in the form of a lawsuit or by telling everyone what a negative experience he or she had with you and your organization. You need to communicate your decision personally and then use the letter as simply a written confirmation of your conversation.

Prepare for the call by writing the specifics you'll communicate from your Interview Planning and Conducting Tool in an outline on the back of your tool. This way all your communications with the person are in the same place, for future reference. If the person calls you to ask about your decision and you need time to prepare, promise to call back in 10 minutes. Then prepare and do it.

Organizations I've worked in that have communicated "We chose another candidate/another person's idea" in this individual way have received thank-you notes from people who've appreciated the communication. The notes always say the same thing: "Thanks for giving me information that'll help me/my company improve."

Acceptance

The basic tenets for communicating acceptance are the same as the ones for rejection:

- Make sure you deliver the news yourself.
- Do it individually by phone or in person and follow up in writing (documentation for candidates for employment/ volunteer work, direct employees, peers and customers, a legal agreement for potential customers and vendors, a visual congratulations for all).
- Be specific about which skills, which attributes of the product or service, which aspects of the idea caused you to decide in their favor. Be specific about how these relate to the job, spec sheet, company mission, or other criteria. Use your Interview Planning and Conducting Tool to get the words; then outline the specifics to communicate.

> **⚠ CAUTION!**
> ## Good News But Bad Approach
> We're all far more comfortable communicating acceptance. Unfortunately, this can cause us to wing it in the conversation. Use your Interview Planning and Conducting Tool to gather the specific words to describe the major points that led to the favorable decision. Write your conversation outline on the tool. Then use it to conduct and document the acceptance conversation, just as you did for the "We chose another candidate/person's idea" conversation.

Some situations for which you need to gain information don't require an accept/reject decision. An example is gathering information from peers or colleagues on best practices or job procedures to be used to develop training or new policies. Though it's not exactly acceptance, the basic tenets still apply:

- Make sure you communicate your decision to them.
- Do it individually by phone or in person and follow up in writing (for recognition and thanks).
- Be specific about what they provided you that made the outcome possible and let them know what the outcome was (a new policy, the new certification program, etc.).

How you communicate acceptance of a person, an idea, or a service or a product affects how a person feels about you and your organization.

Continuously Improving Your Interviewing Skills

The first step in continuously improving your skills is to continuously evaluate them.

Use any one or a combination of the methods below. Choose a method with which you feel comfortable and that doesn't interfere with the conversational quality of the interview.

Methods of Self-Evaluation
- Notice the reactions of the person you're interviewing and make mid-course corrections. (This is the truest definition of "continuously evaluating yourself.")
- Videotape yourself and watch later alone, with a peer, an interviewing coach, and/or your boss.
- Audiotape yourself and listen to later alone, with a peer, an interviewing coach, and/or your boss.
- Have a peer, an interviewing coach, and/or your boss observe you and give you written or verbal feedback.
- Have the person you interviewed give you written or verbal feedback (at the end of the interview or after the decision-making process is completed).

Use this form to get feedback from others or for yourself:
Now that you have this very specific description of what

For each item, write the specific things the interviewer did or said. For the items for which you have no direct evidence from the interview (e.g., choosing the right people to interview, planning for the interview), write the things the interviewer did or said that made you think he/she had done that well or needs to improve:

Used active listening skills

Exhibited "thinking on his/her feet"

Was flexible

Planned for the interview quickly and thoroughly

Organized, compared, and analyzed information

Knew his/her organization/service/product

Believed in his/her organization/service/product

Provided a win-win outcome

Scheduled and followed through carefully and accurately on follow-up

Loves interacting with people

Persisted

Documented thoroughly

Created a good impression for himself/herself and the organization

Helped the person interviewed understand the benefits to him/her

Helped the person interviewed understand what was needed from him/her

Used quick, thorough research skills

Used a voice that the person interviewed interpreted as enthusiastic

Knew the way the person interviewed liked to be communicated with

Understood the time limits of the person interviewed

Spoke and wrote effectively—used words that were clear, was concise, put the subject and verb first, and used the second person ("you")

you did or said relating to each of the interviewer skills, prioritize where you'll start your improvement. You have other things to do, so "continuously improve my interviewing abilities" may be toward the bottom of your list if you find a lot of things to work on.

There are many ways to prioritize. These two methods seem to be favorites:

1. Improve the thing I do poorly that'll be most noticeable and/or most improve my ability to achieve my interviewing objectives.

2. Improve the thing I do poorly that'll be the quickest and/or easiest to change.

These prioritizing methods deal only with the skills that your evaluation shows you need to improve. What about the ones in which you do well?

Intentionally play to your strengths, capitalize on your strengths, and manage around your weakness, Marcus Buckingham and Donald O. Clifton advise in their revolutionary book, *Now, Discover Your Strengths* (New York: Free Press, 2001). The book is based on Gallup Organization research showing that most of us (and our organizations, bosses, and peers) are experts on our weaknesses and we spend our time trying to repair ourselves or others while we do nothing to enhance our strengths. That research found that organizations where a high percentage of people said they felt they had the opportunity every day to do what they do best had a higher percentage of customer loyalty, productivity, and employee retention than others. People were not only using their strengths but working on them.

If you have a weakness that's causing you to not get most of the information you need (no planning, very nervous, can't keep conversational quality), you need to work on it, but you also need to work on your strengths so they become even stronger.

The book reminds us why Tiger Woods is the outstanding golfer he is today: he and his coach practice hard on his strength (an awesome drive) and manage his weakness (sand). In fact he has perfected his drive to such a point that he rarely has to deal with a sand trap—he has developed his strength to such a level that he has virtually eliminated his weakness!

So when you're prioritizing what you'll work on, prioritize using the whole list of feedback on your interviewer skills—the strengths and the weaknesses.

Use the "biggest bang for the buck" and "easiest to imple-ment" prioritizing method. First, rank each of the very specific descriptions of what you did or said relating to each of the inter-viewer skills, based on how easy or hard it will be to work on that strength or weakness. Ignore whether an item is a strength or weakness; just focus on how easy it will be to work on. Rank the items from 1 (easiest) to 20 (hardest).

Then rank each item again, this time based on how noticeable it is and/or how it will improve your ability to achieve your interviewing objectives. (Ignore the first set of numbers.) Use the same scale, from 1 (most noticeable and/or most improve ability to achieve interviewing objectives) to 20 (least).

Now you have your priorities. The interviewer skills with the lowest combined score are the ones to work on first. They'll be easiest and quickest to implement and are the ones that'll be most noticeable and improve your ability to achieve the interviewing objectives! To get ideas for how to enhance the skills you choose, revisit the chapters where those skills are described. (See Chapter 1, pp. 11-12 for a list.) And good interviewing!

Manager's Checklist for Chapter 10

❏ Remove obstacles to using the information you worked so hard to obtain.

❏ When making a decision using the information you gained, you may find you need some clarification. Take the time to get it so you can make the best decision.

❏ Use the information you wrote in your Interview Planning and Conducting Tool to make decisions.

❏ When communicating any decisions or other outcomes of the interviewing process, use messages that leave the person with a positive feeling about you and your organization.

❏ Continuously evaluate your ability to use the successful interviewer skills.

❏ Capitalize on your strengths by continuously seeking a higher level of skill.

❏ Use the chapters of this book as a reference for ideas for improving.

Index

A

Acceptance, communicating, 206–207

Acknowledging receipt of e-mail, 189

Actions, as final step of interviewing, 15–16

Active listening
to deal with anger, 160
overview, 132–134
techniques, 139–148

Additional information, obtaining, 196–200

Addresses, e-mail, 188–189

Advance questions, 9, 95

Agendas, 86–88, 117

Aggressiveness in communication, 168, 171

American Society of Association Executives Web site, 107

Amiables
on assertiveness/responsiveness quadrant, 22, 24
backup style, 36
communicating with other types, 24
expectations of, 39
identifying, 20
questioning style for, 63
recognizing and communicating with, 28–30, 33
stating interview methods for, 124

Analyticals
on assertiveness/responsiveness quadrant, 22, 24
backup style, 37
communicating with other types, 25
expectations of, 39
identifying, 20
questioning style for, 63
recognizing and communicating with, 30–32, 33
stating interview methods for, 124

Anger
as example of difficult behavior, 156–157
possible causes and responses, 160–161

Anti-discrimination laws, 101, 104

Anxiety, 170

Aptitude tests, 10

Arm crossing, 136

Ask assertiveness, 22, 23, 24

"Asking forms," 138

Assertiveness in communication, 22–25, 168–171

Attachments to e-mail, 189–190

Attained objectives, 71

Attention-getting openings, 120

Attitudes, 39–43, 173–174

Audiotape
benefits, 178

Audiotape (*Cont.*)
  guidelines for, 191–192
  for self-evaluation, 207
AV Equipment Checklist, 80, 83
Avoiding truth, 156, 159–160
Awareness, communicating, 43

B
Backup communication styles, 35–37
Bad news, avoiding, 204
Barriers to listening, 148–151
Beginnings
  describing self and organization, 125–127
  First Communication, 87, 88, 120–122
  importance, 109–111
  presenting objectives, 122–124
  stating time and methods, 124–125
  unexpected events, 112–120
Behavior, focus on, 153–154
Behavioral interviewing
  for accurate information, 9–11
  applications, 4–9
  beginning (*see* Beginnings)
  common steps, 12–16
  continuously improving skills, 207–210
  effects of expectations, 161–162
  legal issues, 101–107
  needed skills, 11–12, 19
  overview, 1–4
  questions (*see* Questions)
Beliefs, 39–43
Binary questions, 51–52
Body language
  for active listening, 142–144
  assertive, 170
  to communicate sincerity, 118

effects on communication, 61–66
listening for, 135–136
shortcomings of teleconferences for, 183–184
Breaks in interviews, 162

C
Career planning, 5–6
Casual conversation, 105–106, 114
CHEER model, 140
Chitchat (*see* Casual conversation)
Choices, presenting in questions, 51–52
Clarification methods, 196–200
Clarifying questions, 54–57, 146–147
Clarity, importance in e-mail interviewing, 188
Closed questions, 45–47, 50–52
Coaching, 5–6, 94
Colleagues, 8–9, 201
Comfort with interactions, 118–120
Commitment, 15, 127–130
Communication
  assertive, 22–25, 168–171
  of decisions, 201–207
  needed skills, 19
  overview, 1–2
Communication Style Expectations Tool, 38, 39
Communication Style First Communication Matrix, 120, 121
Communication Style Strategy Sheet, 38
Communication styles
  assessing, 20–21
  backup styles, 35–37
  dimensions, 22–25
  influence of experiences and values, 39–43

Communication styles (*Cont.*)
modifying interview agenda for,
86–87
origins, 21
planning to modify, 38–39
practicing identification, 32–35
recognizing and communicating with, 25–32
word choice and, 138
Computer-assisted interviewing,
179, 184–186
Concentration, in active listening,
140
Conclusions, 15
Confidence, 137, 138, 170
Conflicts, resolving, 172
Consultants, 201
Content focus, 133
Control responsiveness, 23–24
Crossed arms, 136
Culture, 40–41, 151
Current customers
behavioral interviews for, 7–8
information sources about, 95
required decisions about, 201
Customers
behavioral interviews for, 7–8
information sources about, 95
interviews in their workspaces,
85–86
required decisions about, 201

D
Date and time, setting, 81
Debates, avoiding, 205
Decision making
communicating decisions,
201–207
difficulties, 195
as final step of interviewing,
15–16
using information gathered,
200–201

Development Dimensions
International Inc., 2, 57
Difficult behavior
avoiding negative emotions,
171–174
common examples, 155–157
determining causes, 162–171
possible causes and responses,
157–162
right approach to, 153–155
Direct employees (*see* Employees)
Discomfort with technology, 186
Discrimination, 203–204
Distractions
as barriers to listening, 133,
150–151
removing from interview
space, 83
during teleconferences,
181–182
Distractions to Plan Out
Checklist, 81, 84–85
Documents
discussions of, 9–10
excessive, 148
reading at beginning of interview, 116
required retention periods, 107
Drivers
on assertiveness/responsive-
ness quadrant, 22, 24
backup style, 35
communicating with other
types, 24
expectations of, 39
identifying, 20
questioning style for, 63
recognizing and communicating with, 25–27, 33, 34
stating interview methods for,
124

E

Effective listening, 133–134
E-mail, 178, 187–191
Emote responsiveness, 23–24
Emotional trigger words, 149
Empathy, 43, 140, 141
Emphasis, in questioning, 66
Employees
    behavioral interviews for, 5–6
    information sources about, 94
    required decisions about, 200
Employment candidates (*see* Job candidates)
Endings
    gaining commitment, 127–130
    importance, 110, 111
Environment, setting, 78–86
Environment Checklist, 79–80
Equal Employment Opportunity Commission, 103
Excessive information, 156, 158–159
Excessive talking by interviewer, 131–132
Expectations, 161–162
Experiences
    in conjunction with interviews, 10
    as focus of behavioral interviewing, 2
    influence on communication, 39–43
Expressions
    for active listening, 142–144
    assertive, 170
    effects on communication, 61–66
    listening for, 135–136
Expressives
    on assertiveness/responsiveness quadrant, 22, 24
    backup style, 35
    communicating with other types, 24
    expectations of, 39
    identifying, 20
    questioning style for, 63
    recognizing and communicating with, 27–28, 33, 34
    stating interview methods for, 124
Eye contact
    assertive, 170
    guidelines for, 63–64, 136

F

Face-to-face interviewing, 176
Facial expressions
    for active listening, 142–144
    assertive, 170
    effects on communication, 61–62
    guidelines for, 63–64
    listening for, 135–136
Feedback
    in active listening, 146–147
    for self-evaluation, 207–208
Feeling objectives
    creating, 76–78
    defined, 14
    examples, 70
    planning and, 69
    stating at beginning of interview, 123
Fidgeting, 136
Fight-or-flight response, 35–36
Filters, 41–42
First Communication, 87, 88, 120–122
Five why's, 164
Flexibility, 43, 133
Fluidity, 47–50
Fluidity index, 47–50

Focus groups, 113
Follow-up
    acceptance or rejection,
        203–207
    as final step of interviewing,
        15–16
    questions, 53–57
Forms and worksheets
    AV Equipment Checklist, 80, 83
    Communication Style
        Expectations Tool, 38, 39
    Communication Style First
        Communication Matrix, 120,
        121
    Communication Style Strategy
        Sheet, 38
    Distractions to Plan Out
        Checklist, 81, 84–85
    Environment Checklist, 79–80
    Handouts Checklist, 80, 83
    Interview Planning and
        Conducting Tool, 84, 92–93,
        97–101, 196–197, 198–200
    Interviewing Decision
        Worksheet, 201, 202
    Materials Checklist, 81, 84
    Reason for Interviewing First
        Communication Matrix, 120,
        121, 122
    self-evaluation feedback,
        207–208
    Supplies Checklist, 80, 83
Fun in interviews, 155
Furniture, 82

G
Gender differences, 151
General agendas, 86–88, 117
Generalizations, avoiding, 135
Gestures, 64–65
Ginsburg, Charles, 183
Golden Rule, 18

Gut feelings, 103

H
Habits, 139, 144
Handouts Checklist, 80, 83
Hearing, 140
Hemispheric dominance theory,
    115
Hierarchy of laws, 104
Hook, 120
"Hopefully," 137
*How to Read a Person Like a
    Book*, 135
Humor in interviews, 155

I
Information
    determining when sufficient,
        196–200
    excessive, 156, 158–159
    explaining use at end of inter-
        view, 128–129
    insufficient, 156, 159, 195
Information gathering
    communication styles and,
        39–43
    as heart of interviewing, 15
    before interview, 91–93
    methods, 88–90
    obstacles, 194–196
    seeking additional information,
        196–200
    sources, 94
Information objectives
    creating, 75–76
    defined, 14
    examples, 70
    planning and, 69
    stating at beginning of inter-
        view, 122–123
In-person interviewing, 176
Instant messaging, 178, 187–191

Instructions, for technology-based interviews, 185
Insufficient information, 156, 159
Interactions, comfort with, 118–120
Intercultural Competence, 151
Interest, communicating, 43
Interest inventories, 10
Interpretation, 135
Interviewer
  assertiveness, 168–171
  avoiding negative emotions, 171–174
  as cause of difficult behavior in subject, 161–162, 165
  excessive talking, 131–132
  telling subject about, 125–127
Interviewing
  for accurate information, 9–11
  beginning (*see* Beginnings)
  behavioral, 1–9
  common steps, 12–16
  communication style identification, 38–39
  continuously improving skills, 207–210
  effects of expectations, 161–162
  legal issues, 101–107
  needed skills, 11–12, 19
  negative connotations, 3
  questions (*see* Questions)
Interviewing Decision Worksheet, 201, 202
Interview Planning and Conducting Tool
  for acceptance or rejection calls, 205, 206
  planning with, 97–101
  post-interview writing, 84
  pre-interview writing, 92–93
  for seeking clarification, 196–200

Interview preparation (*see* Preparation)
Interview tools (*See also* Technology tools)
  as barriers to listening, 149
  preparing, 96–101
  use without preparing, 117
Interviews, defined, 2

J
Job candidates
  accepting, 206–207
  behavioral interviews for, 4–5
  information sources about, 94
  rejecting, 203–205
  required decisions about, 200

L
Lateness, 113–114
Laughter, nervous, 136–137
Leading questions, 56
Leading teleconferences, 182
Left brain/right brain theory, 115, 157
Legal issues, 101–107
Letters of rejection, 205
Listening
  active, 132–134, 139–148, 160
  barriers to, 148–151
  defined, 140
  importance, 131–132
  objectives, 134–139

M
Mars and Venus in the Workplace, 42, 151
Materials Checklist, 81, 84
"Maybe," 137
Measurable objectives, 71
Methods of interviewing, 88–90
Microphones, 183
Mistakes, 69

Monitors, in videoconferences, 183
Multiple-choice questions, 51
Murphy's Law, 182

N

Negative emotions, avoiding, 171–174
Nervousness
    at beginning of interview, 114–116
    determining causes, 166
    listening for, 136–137
NetMeeting, 184
Nike Retail Division, 179
Nonverbal communication
    for active listening, 142–144
    assertive, 170
    to communicate sincerity, 118
    listening for, 135–136
    shortcomings of teleconferences for, 183–184
    types, 61–66
Note taking, 135, 146–148
Now, Discover Your Strengths, 209

O

Objectives
    of active listening, 134–139
    communicating to interviewees, 72
    defined, 13
    importance, 12, 58
    for interview environment, 78–86
    legal issues, 104–107
    for pre-interview communications, 96
    presenting in beginning, 122–124
    setting, 70–78
    types, 14
Open-ended questions
    defined, 46

examples, 46, 53
    shortcomings, 47
    strengths, 52–53, 54
Open-mindedness, 134
Opinions, 103
Organization, telling subject about, 125–127

P

Pacing the voice, 65
Paragraphs, in e-mail, 188
Paraphrasing
    in active listening, 144–146
    to address various difficult behaviors, 158–159
    to overcome vagueness, 154–155, 158
Parroting, paraphrasing versus, 145
Passiveness in communication, 168
Past behavior, as focus of behavioral interviewing, 2
Pausing
    by interview subjects, 137
    in questioning, 65–66
PDF files, 189–190
Peers
    behavioral interviews for, 6–7
    feedback from, 207
    required decisions about, 200–201
Percentage target, for talking by interviewer, 131–132
Perception filters, 41–42, 60–61
Performance appraisals, 5–6
Performance during interviews, 106
Personal Styles and Effective Performance, 21
Personality, 153–154
Personality tests, 10
Perspective shifting, 42

Planning (*See also* Preparation)
   agenda and methods, 86–90
   benefits, 68–69
   communication styles, 38–39
   elements of, 13–14, 108
   environment, 78–86
   legal issues, 101–107
   setting objectives, 70–78
   time savings from, 97
   tools (*see* Interview Planning
      and Conducting Tool)
   Platinum Rule, 17, 18, 19
Positive attitude, 173–174
"Possibly," 137
Potential customers
   behavioral interviews for, 7–8
   information sources about, 95
   interviews in their workspaces,
      85–86
   required decisions about, 201
Practice
   detecting communication
      styles, 32–35
   listening, 139
   for technology-based inter-
      views, 185
Precedence, of laws, 104
Preparation (*See also* Planning)
   advance communications with
      subject, 93–96
   elements of, 13–14, 108
   interviewing without, 117
   interview tools, 96–101
   legal issues, 101–107
   pre-interview information gath-
      ering, 91–93
Primacy-recency effect, 110
Prioritizing methods, 208–210
Privacy, 82–83
Problem-solving interviews, 10

Q
Questions
   in active listening, 146–147
   closed, 45–47, 50–52
   to deal with anger, 160–161
   defined, 46
   follow-up, 53–57
   open-ended, 46, 47, 52–54
   selecting with STAR, 57–60
   sending to interview subjects in
      advance, 9
   variety and fluidity, 46–50
   ways of asking, 60–66

R
Ranking questions, 51
Reading
   as advantage of e-mail inter-
      views, 190–191
   at beginning of interview, 116
Realistic objectives, 72
Reason for Interviewing First
   Communication Matrix, 120,
   121, 122
Receipt acknowledgement, for e-
   mail, 189
Record-keeping requirements,
   107
References, calling, 94
Refreshments, 84
Rejection, communicating,
   203–205
Repetition, 114–115, 145
Repetitive why analysis, 164–167
Respect, communicating, 42–43
Responsibilities, reviewing,
   129–130
Responsiveness in communica-
   tion, 22–25
Restating objectives, 114–115
Retention requirements for docu-
   mentation, 107

Reviewing responsibilities, 129–130
Rominger Legal Web site, 107
Rooms, planning for, 82–83

S
Safe topics for chitchat, 105–106
Seating, 82
Second opinions, 22
Secondary backup styles, 37
Selection versus rejection, 204
Self-evaluation methods, 207–210
Signatures, electronic, 188
Sincerity, communicating, 118
Situations/Tasks, Actions, and Results (STAR), 57–60
Skills
continuously improving, 207–210
important to interviewing, 11–12
Small talk (*see* Casual conversation)
SMART criteria, 71–73
Social Style/Management Style, 21
Specific objectives, 71, 74
Sperry, Roger, 115
Standardized tests, 10
STAR (Situations/Tasks, Actions, and Results), 57–60
Statement questions, 51, 53, 55
Strengths, improving, 209–210
Stress, backup styles and, 35–37
Style, importance in e-mail interviewing, 188
Subject lines, in e-mail, 188
Superficiality, 155, 158
Supplies Checklist, 80, 83

T
Table mikes, 183

Tables, 82
Talking, excessive, 131–132
Taping interviews, 191–192
Targeted Selection, 2, 57
Teach Yourself Body Language, 135
Technical difficulties, 185–186
Technology tools
audio- and videotape, 178, 191–192
benefits and disadvantages, 176–179
computer-assisted interviewing, 179, 184–186
e-mail and instant messaging, 178, 187–191
overview, 175–176
telephone, teleconferences, and videoconferences, 177, 179–184
webcasts, 178, 184–186
Teleconferences, 177, 179–184
Telephone interviewing, 177, 179–184
Television shows, listening practice, 138–139
Tell assertiveness, 22, 23, 24
Ten keys to effective listening, 133–134
Tests, 10, 62
"Thank-you" following interview, 129–130
Time, as interview objective, 72
Tone of voice, 65–66
Tools (*see* Interview tools)
Tours, 10–11
Travel, overcoming obstacles with technology, 177–178
Trigger words, 149
Truthfulness, avoiding, 156, 159–160

U

Unexpected events
  as barriers to listening,
    150–151
  beginning the interview after,
    112–120
  planning for, 100–101
Unplanned interviews, 78–79

V

Vagueness, 154–155, 158
Values, 39–43
Variety of interview questions,
  46–47
Vendors
  behavioral interviews for, 8–9
  information sources about, 95
  required decisions about, 201
Verbal delivery problems,
  149–150
Videoconferences, 177, 179–184
Videotape
  benefits, 178
  guidelines for, 191–192
  for self-evaluation, 207

Viruses, e-mail, 190
Voice characteristics
  assertive, 170
  guidelines for, 65–66, 136–137
  nervous, 115
Voices of Diversity, 42
Volunteer candidates, 4–5, 200

W

Weaknesses, improving, 209–210
Web sites, 107
Webcasts, 178, 184–186
Willing and Able Chart, 163–164
Woods, Tiger, 209
Words
  assertive, 170–171
  emotional triggers, 149
  importance in e-mail interview-
    ing, 187–188
  listening for, 137–138
Worksheets (*see* Forms and
  worksheets)
World Wide Web, 178, 184–186
Writing, 115

About the Author

Carolyn B. Thompson is President of TRAINING SYSTEMS, INC., a customized performance improvement and HR consulting company in Frankfort, Illinois dedicated to helping small and medium-sized organizations enhance their ability to recruit, inspire, and retain quality employees and improve performance through training (www.trainingsys.com).

She's written articles on employee recruitment, inspiration and retention, interactive training design, and dynamic facilitation skills and contributed a chapter on customers with disabilities to the book, *Americans with Disabilities Act: Access and Accommodations*. She's the editor of the monthly publication *Recruit, Inspire and Retain* and the author of *Creating Highly Interactive Training Quickly and Effectively* (TSI Publications, 2000).

She is a member of the Society for Human Resource Management, the American Society of Association Executives, the International Society for Performance Improvement, the Christian Management Association, and the International Association of Facilitators.

Contact her at 815-469-1162 or e-mail her at CBT@trainingsys.com.